MARCO

BERLIN

with Local Tips

The author's special recommendations are highlighted in yellow throughout this guide

GW00419875

There are five symbols to help you find your way around this guide:

★

Marco Polo's top recommendations

sites with a scenic view

where the local people meet

where young people get together

(A1) *map references*   **(0)** *outside area covered by map*

MARCO ⊕ POLO

Other travel guides and language guides in this series:

Algarve • Amsterdam • Australia • Brittany • California
Channel Islands • Costa Brava/Barcelona • Costa del Sol/Granada
Côte d'Azur • Crete • Cuba • Cyprus • Florence • Florida • Gran Canaria
Greek Islands • Ibiza • Ireland • Istanbul • Lanzarote • Mallorca
Malta • New York • New Zealand • Normandy • Paris • Prague
Rhodes • Rome • Scotland • South Africa • Tenerife
Turkish Coast • Tuscany • Venice

French • German • Italian • Spanish

*Marco Polo would be very interested to hear your
comments and suggestions. Please write to:*

*World Leisure Marketing Ltd
Marco Polo Guides
9 Downing Road, West Meadows
Derby DE21 6HA England*

*Our authors have done their research very carefully, but should any errors or omissions
have occurred, the publisher cannot be held responsible for any injury, damage
or inconvenience suffered due to incorrect information in this guide.*

*Cover photograph: At the Brandenburg Gate (Magazin)
Photographs: Gläser (53, 58); Hotel Kempinski Archive (72); Irrgang (60, 63, 74, 78);
Kallabis (8, 36, 44, 88); Lade: Tzimopulos (19); Mauritius: Elsen (11, 28),
HVH (14, 77, 80, 85), Vidler (4, 35), Waldkirch (inside front cover); K.U. Müller (16, 26);
NBL: Pouier (66); Westerwelle (46); ydo sol (79)*

*1st English edition 1998
© Mairs Geographischer Verlag, Ostfildern Germany
Author: Joachim Nawrocki
Translation: Paul Fletcher
English edition: Cathy Muscat, Emma Kay
Editorial director: Ferdinand Ranft
Design and layout: Thienhaus/Wippermann
Printed in Italy*

CONTENTS

Discover Berlin

The Berlin Wall has gone and the city is resuming its place as capital of a united Germany

Paris, London or Budapest may be more beautiful; Istanbul or Rome may be older; New York or Rio de Janeiro may be more urbane; but no city is as interesting, as politically significant, as much a part of the modern world, as Berlin. Just a few years ago, you could have walked from one economic system to another: from West Berlin's market economy to the planned economy of the communist German Democratic Republic. Now you can witness a unique historical event: the merging of two halves of a divided city, the reunification of Germany, the restoration of Berlin as the capital of a nation at the heart of Europe. This transformation, which began nearly a decade ago, is still ongoing – it will need years, probably decades, to take effect. Thus for the foreseeable future Berlin promises to be an exciting place. Throughout the whole of Greater Berlin, from the grandest boulevard to the ugliest tenement in the

Schloss Charlottenburg and the memorial to the Great Elector

remotest corner, there will be change, upheaval, disappointment and renewal.

As Berlin prepares to resume its place as a great European capital city, the past is once more coming to light. Old buildings, long-standing traditions, and forgotten works of art are emerging from a community which was for so many years cursed by partition, no-go areas, economic mismanagement, decay and the corrosive effects of the Cold War. Intent on parading the validity of their political system and on carving out a distinct national identity, the masters of communist East Berlin denounced, neglected, and often destroyed the old. In West Berlin the authorities indulged the pseudo-modern Zeitgeist, pursuing extravagant modernity rather than preserving what was of historical importance. In the name of architectural prestige and large-scale planning, it was the urban landscape, not the people who populated it, which received the attention. The by-products of these policies were the destruction of viable living spaces and the disappearance of community

History at a glance

c. 8000 BC
First settlement by the Spree

1st to 3rd centuries AD
Germanic tribes settle in the region

1244
First recorded mention of Berlin

1369
Berlin becomes a member of the Hanseatic League

1618-48
Berlin is drawn into the Thirty Years' War. The population, 12 000 in 1618, is halved by plague

1640
Under the Great Elector, Friedrich Wilhelm, commerce flourishes and Berlin is fortified

1710
Berlin's population reaches 56 000

1740-86
Frederick the Great sets out to give Berlin the splendour of a European capital

1806
Napoleon enters Berlin

1838
Rail link with Potsdam opens

1848
Berlin's population reaches 400 000

1871
Berlin becomes capital of a united German Empire

1881
First electric tram

1918
Kaiser Wilhelm abdicates, leading to the first German republic

1920
Greater Berlin's population reaches 4 million

1932-33
Unemployment in the city reaches 636 000. Hitler becomes Chancellor

1936
X Olympiad held in Berlin

9-10 November 1938
Kristallnacht (Night of Broken Glass)

1939-45
Allied air attacks in 1943 devastate the city. In April 1945 the Russians close in on Berlin

1949
Soviets attempt to force the Allies out of Berlin. Giant airlift to sustain the Western sectors

1953
Workers' uprising in East Berlin

1961
The Berlin Wall is built

9 November 1989
The Berlin Wall is breached

1990
Berlin is unified

1991
Bonn parliament resolves to move the federal capital to Berlin by 2000

1994
Russian, British and French forces withdraw

life from Berlin's once-thriving streets and squares.

Fortunately, not everything has been lost. With the collapse of the Wall, once-famous vistas are being restored. With one or two notable exceptions, the East Germans lacked the money to carry out post-war reconstruction and demolition work on the scale they would have liked, and many buildings, which in West Berlin would probably have been torn down, were simply left, such as the Prussian Parliament and the old Scheunenviertel (Barn Quarter). Art historians, architects, and tourists are rediscovering some fascinating sights, not just in Berlin, but also in the surrounding area. Almost every small town has a church or a palace whose style was at least influenced by Schinkel or Persius, or a park which was laid out by Lenné or Pückler. The demise of the communist regime and the collapse of the Wall came just in time for many of these gems to be saved and later to be restored. Ten more years of communism, and much would have been beyond repair.

On the other hand, the war, the planners, and the ideologists have left behind so many gaps in the city's fabric that there is ample room for new buildings – and many will be needed for the increasing administrative functions which will accompany Berlin's role as capital city. Berlin is booming – culturally, economically, politically, and as a tourist destination – and its growth is likely to continue for the foreseeable future. What is emerging resembles the Berlin of the 1920s: a vibrant capital city, a commercial hub, and a bridge between East and West. The scale of the task is such that architects and planners will be kept busy for a century; nevertheless, their work is bound to arouse controversy. Many fear that what is being created is not a seamless join between the two halves of the city, but a self-inflicted wound.

Berlin has already ceased to resemble the place it was before 9 November 1989, when the Wall so quickly and unexpectedly tumbled down. Two totally distinct cities, the walled island and the hated headquarters of an authoritarian power, have changed and fused into one – the streets, the railway lines, the telephones, the police, the fire brigade, the city council and its administrative bodies, the museums and art collections, trade and commerce, gradually the people and their living space in the hinterland too. Only a few fragments of the Wall now remain, like the ruins of a civilization as remote as Carthage or Ancient Rome. Houses that for decades belonged to two different worlds now face each other again, across streets that were once the scene of government-sanctioned murder.

You can now travel around Berlin freely, just like any other city. You can explore the surrounding area, its woodland, its lakes and its suburbs. The city has regained its hinterland. Berlin now feels like a completely different place, and the people have become different too: more self-confident, less restrained, more curious, although occasionally a little sullen and world-weary. West Berlin was like a Surrealist cage. Now, as in the words of contemporary composer György

Where the tombs of the Prussian kings lie: Berliner Dom

Ligety: 'Those inside the cage are free.' And those who were outside the cage are also free, though a surreal atmosphere still persists.

Yet times are changing. 'With the power of a tornado, she sucked in whatever strove upwards in Germany' – so wrote the dramatist Carl Zuckmayer, describing the Berlin of the 1920s. His words are sure to be equally apt for the Berlin of the 21st century. The city will once again become a pool of talent and an intellectual melting pot formed by the collision of East and West; yet the new Berlin need not become a monster, sucking the life-force from Germany's other regional centres. After all, Germany is a federal republic now, and the provincial capitals will not relinquish their importance. Munich, Hamburg and Stuttgart will remain the cultural, commercial and political centres of their regions, and the five new provincial capitals in eastern Germany are already flexing their muscles.

Berlin itself is acquiring a completely new dimension. Until recently, it was the most easterly city in Western Europe, a showpiece for the Western World, an outpost of freedom, a thorn in the flesh of the Eastern Bloc states; now it is also the most westerly city in the East. All of Berlin's previous handicaps – its geographical position, its peculiar political situation, its split cultural identity – are now advantages. Berlin can make a leap forward like no other city, overcome undreamed-of challenges, fascinate people from all over the world. Berlin's magnetism will attract not just politicians, entrepreneurs, journalists and artists, but also tourists, eager to be a part of the action, take advantage of the unbelievable range of cultural events that the undivided city offers, explore Berlin's legendary 'alternative' scene, discover the surrounding area – or simply relax amid Berlin's vast wealth of forests, parkland, lakes and rivers.

Given the current situation, it may seem a little reckless to be writing a guidebook to Berlin, as there is no other city in the world which is undergoing such rapid change. You could decide to visit a popular flea market on a stretch of city-centre wasteland, only to find out that the earth movers and cranes have recently taken over the site. You might read that Kreuzberg or Prenzlauer Berg epitomizes the city's alternative lifestyle, when every day they become more and more gentrified. How can a book recommend a restaurant in eastern

Berlin, when new places open almost daily and just as many overreach themselves and have to close? How long can prices remain valid in the midst of economic upheaval, as a market economy replaces communism? Which theatres will continue to receive subsidies, when there is so much poverty in the new federal states that surround Berlin? Which pictures will be hanging in the art galleries the day after tomorrow, when the collections that were rent asunder by the war are reunited?

So be prepared for changes and surprises, most of which will be pleasant. As the city comes back to life, the normal laws of arithmetic are suspended: one and one make more than two. East and West are getting to know each other again, learning in the process and acquiring new perspectives. When it comes to culture, particularly the alternative culture in both parts of the city, artists are enriching each other's work and reaching new audiences. New galleries are opening in eastern Berlin, bringing hitherto unknown painters and sculptors into the public eye. New pubs and bars are emerging,

often in the unlikeliest of places such as in rear courtyards, tenement blocks or old factories. Young people are arriving in Berlin from all over the world to be a part of what is taking place. They pack the cafés, the rock music pubs and the jazz concerts, and haggle over souvenirs and communist memorabilia in the flea markets.

Many first-time visitors to Berlin are surprised by what they find. It is not just a city of streets lined by bleak tenement blocks, where the traffic comes to a standstill every Friday evening, but also a city with tranquil suburbs, rural areas, wide expanses of woodland and lakes, and many fine man-made landscapes. It is true that the bustle and clamour are increasing, and life is becoming more hectic and more metropolitan as Berlin evolves into a capital, and new government offices fill the skyline. Do not imagine that people are simply reliving the past, reviving the spirit of Kaiser Wilhelm or reawakening Germany's old imperial aspirations, as they speak of how Berlin will gain in political and cultural importance when the parliament and government eventually be-

The Berlin Bear

A bear has featured on Berlin's coat of arms since 1280. Later on, the bear was joined by an eagle, perched on its head. The bear and wall which feature on the present coat of arms was introduced in 1875 – well before the other Berlin Wall came into existence. Despite this, and popular belief that the city's name means something like 'place where bears live', it is unlikely that the name Berlin actually has anything to do with bears at all. The name probably means something a little more prosaic like 'firm place', ie an island of solid land surrounded by marshland or shallow water – which makes sense, given Berlin's watery location.

come established here. The authorities have allowed themselves plenty of time to stage building competitions and make, revise and refine their plans. It is estimated that moving the administration from Bonn to Berlin will take until the year 2000.

As a result of the move, dozens of historic buildings will be brought back to life and, of course, given new functions: the Reichstag, for example, and the Reichstag Presidential Palace opposite; the two buildings which housed the old Prussian Parliament on Leipziger Strasse; the Municipal Offices in Parochial Strasse; the Red Town Hall (so called because of its red brickwork, not its political leanings); the Crown Prince's Palace; the Armoury, and many other buildings in the district surrounding Unter den Linden, the elegant boulevard that is to be restored to its former glory.

There are actually more pre-war buildings here than there might seem to be at first glance. Many of them were hidden in the shadow of the Wall, concealed behind hoardings and derelict sites, or blackened into obscurity by decades of dust and smoke. Tidying these buildings up, and filling the gaps, should be a relatively quick job, and Berlin should soon be able to present much of its former self to the world. At the same time, various reminders of the Nazi era and the resistance movement will be left to serve as a warning of the dangers of national pride: the Gestapo cellar in the former Prinz Albrecht Strasse, the villa by the Wannsee where the decision was made to exterminate the Jews, the memorial to the German resistance movement in Stauffenbergstrasse, the execution site at the Plötzensee, and Schinkel's Neue Wache with its changing exhibitions. Memorials commemorating the years of communist dictatorship and the reign of terror of the secret police (*Staatssicherheitsdienst*, or *Stasi* for short) will also be built, for this is another chapter in Germany's recent history which cannot be forgotten.

In terms of relics from the past Berlin cannot compare with Rome or Paris, but there are more places of historical interest than many people realize. The oldest buildings are the countless village churches, some of which go back to the 13th century; other ancient monuments include the Nikolaikirche in the city centre (1230), parts of the Spandau citadel (c. 1200), the 16th-century Jagdschloss Grunewald, and the Alter Marstall and the Zeughaus, both of which date from the 17th century.

Berlin may not be as ancient as Athens, Istanbul, or even Paris, but around the time that the Romans were founding Cologne on the banks of the Rhine, the Germanic Semnones were establishing settlements in the Berlin region, and their king Masuus went on a state visit to Emperor Domitian in Rome.

A few hundred years later, the Semnones and other Suevian tribes migrated south-west to re-settle by the River Main and in Swabia. Their place by the rivers Spree and Havel was taken by the Burgundi, but in around 650 they too headed westward. Slavonic Wends moved in next, living peacefully alongside the remaining Germanic farmers. The first fortresses were built in Spandau, Köpenick and Brandenburg. Around the year 1100, a new set of German colonists appeared, making their way up from the Lower Rhine regions, establishing numerous settlements, castles, market centres and dioceses. The Holy Roman Emperor Lothar appointed Albrecht the Bear as margrave (ruler of a *Mark* or frontier province) of the area between the Elbe and the Havel.

In Albrecht's domain lay Brandenburg, a town which for centuries had borne the brunt of border warfare; hence his territory came to be known as the Mark Brandenburg.

It was not until 1237 that Cölln on the Spree was first mentioned in documents, followed seven years later by the small settlement on the opposite bank, known as Berlin. In a development mirrored by present-day Berlin, the two towns merged their adminis-

Currently undergoing a futuristic facelift: Potsdamer Platz

trations and finally, in 1432, became an undivided town – until 1948 at any rate. Meanwhile, Emperor Sigismund had appointed the Nuremburg Burgrave Friedrich of Hohenzollern as governor (*Statthalter*) of the Mark Brandenburg. In 1415 he was elevated to the rank of elector (*Kurfürst*) as Friedrich I. His successors were to become Prussian kings and later, German emperors. Friedrich set the pace for his illustrious heirs and, against the wishes of the Berliners, built himself a palace (*Schloss*) on the banks of the Spree. Despite damage in World War II, the Schloss would have stood there to this day, had not the East German government decided to demolish it. In its place, Walther Ulbricht built the almost universally unpopular, and now empty, Palace of the Republic.

The first really important elector was Friedrich Wilhelm, sometimes referred to as the 'Great Elector', who reigned from 1640 to 1688. It was he who created the Brandenburg-Prussian state and made Berlin its capital. His son, Friedrich III, was crowned King Friedrich I of Prussia in Königsberg in 1701. He expanded the town even further and emptied the state coffers of all its funds in the process. His successor, Friedrich Wilhelm I, the 'Soldier King', had little choice but to tighten the town's purse strings. Berlin was to become a working city – never mind the genteel cultural preoccupations of his son, later crowned King Friedrich II. Friedrich Wilhelm was much more interested in building factories for the manufacture of uniforms and armaments, furthering trade, and developing financial institutions and the construction industry. The city developed suburbs, and Bohemian immigrants arrived in Berlin and Rixdorf, following in the path of the 6000 Huguenots (French Protestants) who had found refuge from persecution there 50 years previously. When Friedrich II (1740–86) finally acceded to the throne, he fostered German culture and the sciences, as well as encouraging the cotton and silk manufacturing industries, buying the porcelain manufacture which exists to this day, and employing skilful warfare to turn Prussia into a great, if rather unpopular, European power. These achievements earned Friedrich the epithet 'der Grosse', or in English, 'Frederick the Great'.

'Old Fritz' (as he was less flatteringly known) may have been an enlightened monarch, but that did not stop his erstwhile subjects giving vociferous support to the French Revolution after his death. Thereafter the Romantic Movement gained an ardent following in Berlin, under the influence of such figures as Achim von Arnim, Ludwig Tieck and Heinrich von Kleist, and the literary salons of Rahel Varnhagen and Henriette Herz. These figures dominated the intellectual climate, which was little affected by the Napoleonic occupation. In the year after the return of the royal court and the state government from Königsberg in 1809, Wilhelm von Humboldt established Berlin University, and soon the institution was flourishing. There followed the golden era of the architect Karl Friedrich Schinkel, the sculptor

Christian Daniel Rauch, and the landscape gardener Peter Joseph Lenné, who all played a part in transforming Berlin and its surrounding area, providing much of the character which survives to the present day.

The early years of the Industrial Revolution had a dramatic impact on the city too. In 1815 Freund and Egells opened the first mechanical engineering works; in 1821 Beuth established a trade institute; 1826 saw the first gasworks, 1837 Borsig, 1847 Siemens and Halske. Berlin had become an industrial city with a large working class, which soon wanted a say in how things were run: in 1848, artisans, students, and workers joined forces at the barricades in a struggle for a liberal constitution, causing the weak King Friedrich Wilhelm IV to issue his appeal 'To my dear Berliners'. But Berlin's industry was rapidly outgrowing the city. In the middle of the 19th century, a new settlement was founded in Moabit on the outskirts, followed at the turn of the century by another at Tegel and, at the same time, a third settlement, now called Siemensstadt, in the vacant space between Charlottenburg and Spandau.

In 1871 Berlin became capital of the German Reich. 1888 was the year of the three Kaisers: Wilhelm I died, followed shortly by his successor, the 'Hundred-Day Kaiser' Friedrich III, and then Wilhelm II came to power. He immediately fell out with Bismarck, and began the militarist expansion which led in due course to World War I. On 9 November 1918, 71 years to the day before the Berlin Wall came down, he went into exile.

Ironically enough, Germany's defeat in World War I was followed by Berlin's finest decade, combining a cultural flowering with strident economic growth, although marred by unregulated speculation and increasing social tension. In 1920 the outlying suburbs were incorporated into the district of Greater Berlin, a city of 3.9 million inhabitants. At the same time, the city was divided into 20 new administrative *Bezirke* (boroughs).

Berlin's demise, however, began in 1933 and, without doubt, the 12 years that followed were the worst in its history. That same year, Hitler seized power and his storm troopers marched through the Brandenburg Gate holding flags and torches aloft. Three years later, the X Olympiad took place in Berlin, with Hitler using the event for Nazi propaganda. One night in November 1938 Nazi supporters took to the streets, vandalizing and destroying Jewish synagogues, shops and other properties in what became known as *Kristallnacht* (Night of Broken Glass). World War II began in 1939 in an atmosphere of optimistic nationalism. However, Nazi triumphalism turned sour when, on 23 November 1943, prolonged air attacks devastated the German capital, which before long lay in ruins. In 1945 the Russians began their land attack, overrunning the city on May 2. On 5 June the four Allied commanders assumed control and divided the city into four sectors.

The initial unity of the occupying forces quickly evaporated. Allied Command and the Allied Control Council soon ceased to function effectively, and the cur-

Schinkel's Schauspielhaus and the Französischer Dom, overlooking the Gendarmenmarkt

rency reform of 1948 provided the Soviets with an excuse for cordoning off West Berlin, thereby dividing the city. The blockade lasted 11 months, and the citizens of the Western sectors had to be supplied by an air bridge. On 16 June 1953 an uprising against the communist regime started in East Berlin, but was brutally put down by Soviet troops. In 1958 Nikita Khrushchev thought he could drive out the Western powers with an ultimatum, but the American president, John F. Kennedy, stood firm.

In order to stem the tide of refugees into West Berlin, the communists had only one option: the construction of a wall. On 13 August 1961, West Berliners woke up to find that their half of the city had been sealed off. Rail links between east and west were severed. But this desperate measure did not bring stability to the East German regime. Economic problems mounted and, despite the Berlin Agreement of 1972

which enabled West Berliners to visit the East and travel in the GDR, the German people refused to accept the political realities of partition.

When Mikhail Gorbachev came to power in Moscow during 1985, the German Communist Party (SED) made it clear that it would continue on its hardline course, if necessary against the will of the reformer in the Kremlin. East Germans were none too impressed by their leaders' intransigence. The GDR might well have been the most successful economy in the Eastern Bloc, but living conditions were far behind those in the West. In 1989 thousands of GDR citizens started to leave via Hungary, where the borders had opened in June. The message these refugees were giving the government in East Berlin was beamed into the living rooms of all East Germans by West German broadcasters, but the SED leadership would not be deflected from its chosen course. Opposition groups under the 'New Forum' banner called for a dialogue with the government and, within weeks, hundreds of thousands of demonstrators were taking to the streets on a regular basis.

It was obvious to all that the Soviet Union was not going to intervene. What was not certain was how much dissent the German communists would allow. Despite some tense moments, the demonstrations remained peaceful. On 18 October, Erich Honecker, the head of the SED and the East German state, resigned. The job of clinging on to power was left to Egon Krenz, up until then the minister for security matters. But the communists had never been prepared to compromise, and Krenz was unwilling to enter into negotiations with New Forum, hoping instead that things would eventually quieten down. On 4 November 1989, a million East Berliners demonstrated on the Alexanderplatz. Broadcast live on East German television, the message was unequivocal: the citizens of the GDR wanted the same rights as West Germans. When the Politburo finally resigned five days later, an announcement was made that the laws restricting travel had been lifted, and hordes of jubilant protesters surged past the border guards who had for the previous 29 years been under instructions to shoot escapees.

On 3 October 1990 Berlin was formally reunified, and new elections took place on 2 December. This peaceful revolution, in which no shot was fired, is a testimony to the people who live here: quiet, patient, intelligent, courageous, and never to be underestimated. Finally, in 1994, Allied and Soviet forces withdrew from Berlin.

Throughout history Berlin has been home to exiles and outcasts: Huguenots, Bohemians, and Silesians all settled here. They were all in some way asylum seekers, treated first with suspicion but then integrated. Berliners have always prided themselves on their special qualities. They are open-minded and tolerant, but newcomers to their city who start making demands will quickly be given the brush-off. Berliners are proud people and have little time for superior attitudes. There are no hierarchies in Berlin, no high society, no political class, no underclass. If you look beyond the bricks and mortar, and show an interest in the people and the atmosphere in which they thrive, you will find it easy to gain access into their lives.

In the Marco Polo Spirit

Marco Polo was the first true world traveller. He travelled with peaceful intentions forging links between the East and the West. His aim was to discover the world, and explore different cultures and environments without changing or disrupting them. He is an excellent role model for the 20th-century traveller. Wherever we travel we should show respect for other peoples and the natural world.

Exploring the city

Berlin is a city of rivers and lakes, boasting more bridges than Venice and longer shorelines than the Côte d'Azur

Berlin is far too sprawling and complex a city to get to know in just a few short exploratory walks. Greater Berlin – with its population of 3.5 million and its area of 880 sq km – stretches 38 km from north to south and 45 km from east to west.

A good place to embark on your voyage of discovery is the Kurfürstendamm. Stroll down the wide avenue, veer off into some of the side streets, and take in the atmosphere around the Sophienkirche and the Neue Synagoge. Another 'must' is the restored end of Unter den Linden, Berlin's answer to the Champs Elysées. On this fine boulevard, whose name translates as 'Beneath the Linden Trees', it is easy to imagine just how beautiful old Berlin was – and how it may well be again in the not too distant future.

But do not be misled into thinking that this is the 'real' Berlin. The more authentic areas are not to be found in the city centre. Take a walk through the 'Charlottenburger Kiez' to the south of Charlottenburg Palace, through Rixdorf with the remains of its Bohemian colony, past the decaying, but still fashionable, tenements of Prenzlauer Berg, or through the part of the city often described as 'Little Istanbul', between Kottbusser Tor and Schlesisches Tor. These parts of the city are inhabited by ordinary, working Berliners.

On the outskirts of the city, around Kolk and Behnitz in Spandau, you are still well within the boundaries of Greater Berlin, but you can get a good impression of what all the towns of Brandenburg must have looked like before being desecrated under the communist regime.

In fact, many of Berlin's real gems lie well away from the bustle of the city centre: the palace and gardens of Charlottenburg; the Pfaueninsel (Peacock Island) with its white-brick folly; the Tierpark (East Berlin's zoo) and Friedrichsfelde palace; Tegeler Fliess; the Schlossinsel at Köpenick and, of course, the innumerable lakes and vast areas of woodland, ideal for long, tranquil walks.

The romantic folly on 'Peacock Island'

Kurfürstendamm (C-D 5)

✪ ⚹ Lined with expensive boutiques, luxury hotels and smart restaurants, for decades the 'Ku'damm' served as a showcase for the West. Its 52 m width was set by Bismarck, who wanted Berlin to have a grand thoroughfare that could compete with the Champs Elysées in Paris. However, over the years the face of this 3 km long boulevard has changed dramatically. In recent times it has lost some of its glamour: fast-food outlets, cheap clothes shops and street traders now compete with the old-established stores. The side streets, such as Bleibtreustrasse and Schlüterstrasse, are actually much more fashionable. Nevertheless, enjoying a cup of coffee and a slice of cake in Café Kranzler or one of the many other pavement cafés along the busy Ku'damm is an essential part of any trip to Berlin.

Back in the 16th century, this wide avenue was little more than a bridle path for the Elector and his entourage to ride from the palace to the Grunewald hunting lodge. By the turn of this century, it was an elegant thoroughfare lined by superb town houses. Sadly, only 40 of them survived World War II.

Charlottenburg; Underground station: Kurfürstendamm

MARCO POLO SELECTION: SIGHTSEEING

1 Funkturm
Berlin's symbolic landmark, offering a great view of the city (page 27)

2 Glienicker Park
Classicism and Romanticism, half way between Berlin and Potsdam (page 30)

3 Kulturforum
The best and the worst of post-war architecture (page 27)

4 Marienkirche
The second-oldest parish church in the city, features a fascinating *Dance of Death* frieze (page 22)

5 Pfaueninsel
A journey back in time to the days of Friedrich Wilhelm II (page 31)

6 Gendarmenmarkt
One of Europe's finest squares (page 34)

7 Reichstag
When the current renovation work is finished, it will once again be the seat of the German parliament (page 28)

8 Schloss Charlottenburg
Once the country lodge of Sophie Charlotte, now a grand palace (page 31)

9 Unter den Linden
Berl'n's historic boulevard is lined with trees and imposing buildings (page 19)

10 Zitadelle Spandau
A 16th-century fortress with a 12th-century tower (page 30)

'Berlin' – street sculpture by Brigitte and Martin Matschinsky-Denninghoff

Unter den Linden (G 4)

★ ☺ This, the most celebrated of Berlin's thoroughfares, is lined by a whole series of imposing buildings. The oldest date from the time of the Prussian kings Friedrich I and Friedrich II – although almost all were rebuilt in the post-war era. The avenue's name translates as 'Beneath the Linden Trees' – after the trees planted by the Great Elector in 1647, to line the route from his palace to his hunting grounds in the Tiergarten. The trees that stand here today were planted after World War II.

A stroll along historic Unter den Linden should really start at the Brandenburger Tor (Brandenburg Gate), which celebrated its 200th anniversary in 1991. The last surviving city gate of an original 18, it was built by Carl G. Langhans in the style of the Propylaeum, the entrance to the Acropolis in Athens. The chariot that tops the gate, known as the Quadriga, was the creation of Johann G. Schadow.

Pariser Platz, to the north, is currently being rebuilt, partly in modern, partly in original style. On the right-hand side stands the Russian embassy, an example of the *Zuckerbäckerstil* or 'wedding-cake style' characteristic of Soviet architecture. A little further on is the Staatsbibliothek (1903–14), the former Prussian state library. This grandiose building, patched up after wartime damage, houses over 3 million volumes. Many of its readers are students from the Humboldt University next door, originally built (1749–1766) as a palace for Frederick the Great's brother, Prince Heinrich. In 1810 it was converted into Berlin University by Wilhelm Humboldt – and later renamed in his honour. Alumni of the Humboldt University have included such celebrated figures as Karl Marx, Friedrich Engels, Karl Liebknecht, the philologists Jacob and Wilhelm Grimm (better known for their fairy tales), and such great scientists as Albert Einstein, Robert Koch and Max Planck. On the opposite, southern side of Unter den Linden stands the Alte Bibliothek (Old Library, 1775–80) with its elegantly curved Baroque façade. In 1895 Lenin came here to study books that were not available to him in Russia. Across the broad expanse of

Bebelplatz stands the Deutsche Staatsoper (National Opera House), built by Knobelsdorff (1741–43) in the style of a Corinthian temple. Further along on the same side of the avenue are the Opernpalais and the Kronprinzenpalais, both designed in the 18th century, but completely rebuilt during the 1960s. Across the road is Schinkel's Neue Wache (New Guardhouse, 1817–18), now a memorial to victims of war and tyranny. A little further on is the Zeughaus – the former armoury – the largest surviving Baroque building from the time of King Friedrich I. Begun in 1695 by Nehring, continued by Grünberg and Schlüter, it was finished in 1706 by Jean de Bodt. Of particular interest inside are Schlüter's vivid and moving reliefs, which depict the faces of dying warriors. The Zeughaus now houses the Deutsches Historisches Museum (History Museum).

Mitte; S-Bahn station: Unter den Linden

BRIDGES

It is often said that Berlin has more bridges than Venice, but it has to be admitted that few can compare with those that grace the Italian city. However, there are three of particular interest:

Glienicker Brücke (0)

Glienicker Bridge links Berlin with Potsdam. Until early 1990 its use was restricted to the Allied forces. It became a frequent sight on TV screens during the Cold War, as this was the spot where East and West exchanged spies.

Königsweg, Wannsee; S-Bahn station: Wannsee, then bus 116

Jungfernbrücke (H 4)

This drawbridge, spanning the southern arm of the Spree, has survived almost unaltered since 1798. The 'Maidens' Bridge' is still raised to allow boats to pass.

Werderscher Markt, Mitte; Underground station: Spittelmarkt

Schlossbrücke (G–H 3)

Built between 1821 and 1824 to plans drawn up by Schinkel, the Palace Bridge was designed to connect Unter den Linden with the Schlossplatz. Dolphin, merman and sea horse motifs decorate the cast-iron balustrades. Lining each side of the bridge are classical statues of warriors and winged figures made from Carrara marble.

Unter den Linden, Mitte; Underground station: Hausvogteiplatz; S-Bahn station: Hackescher Markt

CEMETERIES

Dorotheenstädtischer Friedhof (G 3–4)

This attractive little cemetery lies close to the Brecht-Haus, where the playwright lived and worked from 1953 to 1956. Both he and his wife, Helene Weigel, are buried here. Many artists and academics lie interred in this graveyard, dating from 1762.

Chausseestrasse 126, Mitte; Underground station: Oranienburger Tor

Hallesches Tor Friedhöfe (G 5)

Originally intended for the burial of paupers and Bohemian immigrants, once these cemeteries had been extended and smartened up they attracted the attention of many prosperous families. Now they are amongst the most important in Berlin. The beautiful and bizarre gravestones and mausoleums reflect the lifestyle of Berlin's bourgeoisie during the reign of Frederick the Great. Among the illustrious German figures buried here are the composer Mendelssohn and his family, the writer E.T.A Hoffmann, and the poet and biographer Adalbert von Chamisso.

Mehringdamm or Zossener Strasse, Kreuzberg; Underground station: Hallesches Tor

Invalidenfriedhof (F 3)

Laid out originally in 1748 for the crippled veterans from the nearby refuge for invalids, after the Wars of Independence (1813–15) it became the last resting place for Prussian officers. Its most famous gravestone belongs to General von Scharnhorst, who played a part in the defeat of Napoleon at Leipzig in 1813, and died in the same year in Prague from a wound received in battle.

Scharnhorststrasse 33, Mitte; Underground station: Schwartzkopfstrasse

Jüdischer Friedhof Weissensee (O)

Beyond the entrance to the largest Jewish cemetery in Europe stands a memorial dedicated 'to our murdered brothers and sisters 1933–45'. It takes the form of a circle of tablets bearing the names of all the large concentration camps. Some 120 000 people are buried within this huge area, which was opened in 1880 after the Schönhauser Allee cemetery had been filled to capacity. A walk through here is certainly a moving experience.

Many of the stones are overgrown and only visible through a thick undergrowth – the present Jewish community is too small

and too poor to employ gardeners. What is striking is the contrast between the simple gravestones and the splendid, often extravagant, family vaults. Among the dead buried here is the resistance fighter, Herbert Baum. Just to the right of the entrance lie the Torah scrolls desecrated by the Nazis. Men are only allowed into the cemetery if their heads are covered. The cemetery attendant will provide a cap for a small fee.

Sun–Thurs 08.00–16.00 (winter), 08.00–17.00 (spring), 08.00–18.00 (summer), Fri 08.00–15.00, closed on Jewish holidays; Herbert-Baum-Strasse 45, Weissensee; S-Bahn station: Greifswalder Strasse; Tram: 2, 3, 4, 13

Stahnsdorfer Friedhof (O)

On the south-western outskirts of the city. Of special interest for its many mausoleums and the Nordic wooden church.

Bahnhofstrasse, Stahnsdorf; Bus: 623 from Zehlendorf S-Bahn station

Dorfkirche Marienfelde (O)

The oldest of Berlin's 50 or so surviving village churches. Built around 1220 on the village green, which is still surrounded by farmhouses. A fine example of medieval church architecture.

Alt-Marienfelde, Tempelhof; S-Bahn station: Buckower Chaussee

Friedrichwerdersche Kirche (G 4)

This place of worship, completed in 1830, is reckoned to be Schinkel's most important sacred building. The neo-Gothic brick structure set the tone for church building in Prussia during the 19th century. Badly damaged during World War II, it was restored during the 1980s. It now houses the Schinkel Museum, documenting the life and works of the great architect.

Tues-Sun 09.00–17.00; Werderstrasse, Mitte; Underground station: Hausvogteiplatz

Kaiser-Wilhelm-Gedächtniskirche (E 4)

❖ ✠ All that remains of what must once have been a splendid neo-Romanesque church is the ruined tower. It was built in the 1890s by Franz Schwechten in memory of Wilhelm I, who died in 1888. The partially restored mosaics in the interior reveal some of the Wilhelmine pomp of the original building. The modern octagonal chapel next door was designed by Egon Eiermann and consecrated in 1961.

Organ recitals: Sat 18.00; Breitscheidplatz, Charlottenburg; Underground station: Kurfürstendamm or Zoologischer Garten

Marienkirche (H 3)

★ Dating originally from the 13th century, the church was destroyed in the great fire of 1380. However, it was rebuilt and re-opened in 1405. The tower was added by Carl Gotthard Langhans in 1789. The 15th-century *Dance of Death* frieze, just inside the entrance, and the marble pulpit by Andreas Schlüter (1703) merit closer inspection.

Karl-Liebknecht-Strasse, Mitte; Underground and S-Bahn station: Alexanderplatz

Neue Synagoge (G 3)

When it was finished in 1866, this 3200-seat synagogue was the largest in the world. The Berlin Jewish community at that time numbered about 18 000 members, and was continuing to grow as more and more Jews arrived in the city from eastern Europe. Present at the opening ceremony was Bismarck himself.

This impressive brick-built structure, the work of Eduard Knoblauch and Friedrich August Stüler, was enthusiastically received by the Berlin newspapers at the time of its consecration. One critic wrote: 'A fairy-tale building which, with its light columns, bold arches, colourful arabesques and its diverse and enchanting Moorish-style wood carvings conjures up visions of a modern-day Alhambra.' The effect was enhanced by a conspicuous gilt and turquoise dome.

The synagogue survived the pogroms of the pre-war years with only slight damage. Ironically, it was the Allied bombing attacks of 1943 that reduced it to rubble. Work began on restoring the façade in 1988, and the synagogue was reconsecrated on 6 September 1991, exactly 125 years after its predecessor was finished. The dome, visible from far and wide, has once again become an important Berlin landmark. Next door are the headquarters of the city's Jewish community.

Sun–Thur 10.00–18.00, Fri 10.00–14.00; Oranienburger Strasse 30, Mitte; Underground and S-Bahn station: Oranienburger Strasse; Tram: 1, 13

St-Hedwigs-Kathedrale (G 4)

Erected in 1747, this domed cathedral is reminiscent of the Pantheon in Rome. The idea for such a grand sacred building came from Friedrich II, who wished to demonstrate his religious tolerance. Jean Legeay and

Johann Boumann were responsible for its design and construction. The reliefs date from the 19th century. Reduced to a shell in 1943, the cathedral was not rebuilt until 1963.

Mon–Sat 10.00–17.00, Sun 13.00–17.00; Bebelplatz, Mitte; Underground station: Hausvogteiplatz

Sophienkirche   (G–H 3)

Queen Sophie Luise laid the foundation stone in 1712, Berlin's only surviving Baroque church tower dates from the 1730s, the pulpit from 1712 and the font from 1741. The surrounding area, known as the Spandauer Vorstadt (Spandau suburb) with Sophienstrasse and Grosse Hamburger Strasse, is worth exploring.

Grosse Hamburger Strasse 29, Mitte; Underground station: Weinmeisterstrasse

Synagoge Rykestrasse   (H 3)

Like many of Berlin's synagogues, this was built in a rear courtyard (1904). This is probably why it was spared the Nazi torch, as the adjoining apartments would also have gone up in flames. During the war it was used as a weapons store and stables. Restored in the post-war years, it was reconsecrated in 1953. The capacity of this fine brick structure now easily exceeds the size of the Jewish community in eastern Berlin.

Rykestrasse 53, Prenzlauer Berg; Underground station: Senefelderplatz

DISTRICTS

Charlottenburger Kiez   (C–D 4)

❖ This district to the south of Schloss Charlottenburg, between Sophie-Charlotten-Strasse and Wilmersdorfer Strasse, was the subject of many works by the Berlin painter, Heinrich Zille. Zille produced earthy satirical drawings around the turn of the century. 'Pinsel Heinrich' (Paintbrush Henry), as he was affectionately known, lived in Sophie-Charlotten-Strasse from 1892 until his death in 1929. Using a camera and a sketch pad, he skilfully captured the drudgery of the day-to-day lives of ordinary people. The Kiez survived World War II relatively unscathed, but then had to wait a long time before it received a facelift. Many small businesses still operate from the courtyards behind the ornate façades, but there are also a lot of smart bars and restaurants serving international cuisine in this quarter. Worth seeking out is

---

No more heroes

The GDR loved to honour its heroes – the communist leaders were desperate to instil a sense of pride into their doubting subjects. Schlossplatz (Palace Square) was renamed Marx-Engels-Platz, but the authorities were greatly embarrassed when a dissident sprayed the slogan 'This was not what we wanted' over a statue of the two great men. Lenin's statue was removed long ago, and Ho-Chi-Minh-Strasse and several other streets dedicated to communist leaders have been renamed. If you use an old map to find your way around former East Berlin, chances are you'll get very lost!

the Luisenkirche on Gierckeplatz – like so many of Berlin's buildings, the church tower (1821) bears Schinkel's trademark.
Charlottenburg; Underground station: Bismarckstrasse

Hansa-Viertel (E–F 3)

The Hansa-Viertel to the north of the Tiergarten was bombed out of existence in World War II – creating a blank canvas upon which leading architects could realize their concepts for a modern living space. The resulting new district, built for the International Building Exhibition of 1957 between Strasse des 17 Juni and the S-Bahn, was an imaginative blend of low-rise and high-rise tenement blocks. Among the architects who contributed to the exhibition were Walter Gropius, Pierre Vago, Alvar Aalto, Egon Eiermann, Oscar Niemeyer and Werner Düttman (who also designed the nearby Akademie der Künste on Hanseatenweg).
Tiergarten; Underground station: Hansaplatz

Kreuzberg (H–I 5)

✠ With the demolition of the Wall, the avant-garde district of Kreuzberg found that it had moved from the outer fringes to the centre of the city. Take the route along the Landwehrkanal, from Baerwaldstrasse across the meadows past Urbanhafen, along Planufer and then Maybachufer with its Turkish market, cross the canal at some point and then walk back along the other side, via Paul-Lincke-Ufer and Fraenkelufer to Böcklerpark. You will see more of the real Berlin here than anywhere else in the city: the old and the new, the decaying and the restored, the beautiful and the ugly, Turkish snack bars and trendy pubs. This is the real Kreuzberg.
Underground station: Prinzenstrasse

Märkisches Viertel (0)

Work on this controversial satellite town, now housing a population of around 100 000, started in around 1962 and carried on into the 1970s. The main objections were the large number of vast tower blocks, poor traffic links, and an inadequate infrastructure. Nevertheless, there are people who allegedly like living here, even in the 100-m concrete bunker known as 'Langer Jammer' or 'Long Misery'.
Reinickendorf; S-Bahn station: Wittenau

Marzahn (0)

The socialist counterpart to the Märkisches Viertel is the new town of Marzahn. Some 116 000 people now live in what was once just a quiet village – all that remains are the old village green and a church built in 1871 by Friedrich August Stüler. Most of the present inhabitants were GDR civil servants, hence the local electoral popularity of the repackaged communists, the Democratic Socialist Party.
Marzahn; S-Bahn station: Marzahn

Nikolai-Viertel (H 4)

❦ Berlin grew up around what is the oldest church in the city, the 13th-century Nikolaikirche, in the area now circumscribed by Schlossplatz and Mühlendamm, the River Spree and the Rotes Rathaus. Almost all of the 'old' buildings in this quarter were rebuilt during the 1980s; unfortunately, GDR-style prefab construction techniques were used. In fact, so few of the buildings faithfully follow the original that this quarter is a kind of Disneyland of old Berlin. 'Zum Nussbaum', the pub where the famous Berlin artist Heinrich Zille drank, is a reconstruction. The same is true of the Gerichtslaube, the medieval courthouse (now a restaurant). The original was dismantled in 1870 to make way for the Rotes Rathaus: it was removed to the grounds of Schloss Babelsberg, where it stands to this day. The statue of St George and the Dragon also stood elsewhere. The Knoblauch-Haus (1764) survived the war just about intact, and so ranks as the only truly historic dwelling in the quarter. Once the grand home of a wealthy silk merchant, it now houses an archive that focuses on the Berlin Enlightenment.

The Ephraim-Palais was once considered 'the finest corner in Berlin' and is one of the Nikolai-Viertel's principal attractions. The banker Veitel Ephraim, who was mint master to Frederick the Great, had the house built on Mühlendamm between 1761 and 1767. In 1935, Mühlendamm had to be widened and so the town house was dismantled one stone at a time. The 2493 individual sections were kept in West Berlin until 1983 and then returned to the east of the city to be incorporated into the reconstruction, not far from the building's original location.

Many new restaurants, pubs and specialist shops have recently opened up in the quarter.
Mitte; Underground station: Kloster-strasse

Prenzlauer Berg (H 2–3)

⚹ Much the same as Kreuzberg was a couple of years ago, this old working-class district is ripe for gentrification. But until the clean-up process sets in, it will continue to be a centre for alternative cultures and lifestyles. It stands in what used to be East Berlin and, even then, it had a reputation as a vibrant and exciting corner of the city, with many artists and non-conformist groups just managing to stay on the right side of the authorities. Now, after reunification, hundreds of decaying flats stand empty or are occupied by squatters who have been moved out of squats in West Berlin. Punks and skinheads occasionally square up for street battles. Outlandish bars occupy rear courtyards and attract new Bohemians. For a glimpse of what the revamped district will end up looking like, take a walk around Kollwitzplatz and Husemannstrasse. The much-vaunted renovation project was initiated in the Honecker era, but they did not quite manage to finish the whole street. There are one or two good restaurants here, a tiny hairdressing museum and some corner shops.
Underground stations: Rosa-Luxemburg-Platz, Senefelder Platz

FOUNTAINS

Märchenbrunnen (I 3)

With its statues of characters from the Grimm fairy tales, this huge neo-Baroque arcade and fountain (1913) in Volkspark Friedrichshain will evoke nostalgic childhood memories for many of
Am Friedrichshain/F Friedrichshain; Undergro Rosa-Luxemburg-Platz

Neptunbrunnen (H 3–4)

Kaiser Wilhelm II had this fountain built in the third year of his reign (1888–1918) with the aim of improving the appearance of Schlossplatz. Neptune sits, trident in hand, on a huge shell, surrounded by four female courtiers, symbolizing what were at the time Germany's most important rivers: the Rhine, the Vistula, the Oder and the Elbe. In 1969 the fountain was renovated and moved to its current position in front of the Rotes Rathaus.

Rathausstrasse, Mitte; Underground and S-Bahn station: Alexanderplatz

Weltkugel-Brunnen (E 4)

❀ ⚹ On the bustling Breitscheidplatz, between the Kaiser Wilhelm Gedächtniskirche and the Europa Center, stands a granite globe fountain designed by Joachim Schmettau. Its correct name is the Weltkugel-Brunnen (Globe Fountain), but Berliners refer to it irreverently as the Wasserklops or 'water meatball'.

Breitscheidplatz, Charlottenburg; Underground station: Zoologischer Garten

---

HISTORIC BUILDINGS & MONUMENTS

AEG Turbine Factory (D 3)

Peter Behrens, an important industrial architect of his time, built the turbine assembly shop in 1909. His style was groundbreaking: this was the first time a building's structural elements were designed as an integral part of its exterior. Behrens also designed the AEG factories in Voltastrasse and Hussitenstrasse in the district of Wedding.

Huttenstrasse 12–17, Tiergarten; Underground station: Turmstrasse

Charité (F–G 3)

This hospital was founded in 1710 to house plague victims, and is Berlin's oldest. The oldest surviving part of the building is the smallpox hospital, which dates from 1836. Most of the wards in this vast complex were built in neo-Gothic style around the turn of the century. The new multi-storey hospital block, built between 1977 and 1982, can be seen from miles around.

Schumannstrasse 20–21, Mitte; Underground station: Oranienburger Tör; Bus: 147

The Neptune Fountain

Corbusier-Haus (A 4)

Built on stilts as part of the International Building Exhibition at the end of the 1950s, this residential block consists of 17 floors and 557 mainly two-storey flats. These dwellings open on to nine gloomy internal corridors which resemble the inside of a local authority office block. The building was based on similar designs in the French cities of Marseille and Nantes, but deviated so much from the original plans that its celebrated architect, Le Corbusier, distanced himself from the completed project.

Reichssportfeldstrasse, Charlottenburg; Underground station: Olympia-Stadion

Fernsehturm (H 3)

◁!▷ Built between 1966 and 1969 when the area around Alexanderplatz was being redesigned by the communist authorities, this 365-m TV tower is one of the tallest structures in Europe, but falls tactfully short of its 533-m comrade in the Soviet motherland. Inside the globe at a height of 207 m is a café, affording a fine all-round view of the city as it rotates slowly about its axis.

Daily 10.00–01.00; live music Tues–Sat from 19.00; Panoramastrasse 1a, Mitte; underground and S-Bahn station: Alexanderplatz

Funkturm (B 4)

★ ◁!▷ This 138-m radio tower, little brother to the Eiffel Tower, went into operation just in time for the third German Radio Exhibition, which opened on 4 September 1926. The restaurant is at 55 m, so if you want to see the view before dinner, take the lift to the viewing platform at 126 m.

The Deutsches Rundfunkmuseum (Radio Museum) is situated at the foot of the tower, and puts the development of radio and TV into a socio-historical context.

Tower: Daily 10.00-23.00;
Restaurant: from 11.30;
Museum: Wed–Mon 10.00–17.00; Messedamm entrance, Hammarskjöldplatz 1, Charlottenburg; Underground station: Kaiserdamm; S-Bahn station: Witzleben

Gipsformerei Berlin (C 4)

Moulds for casting copies of the world's great sculptures have been stored here since 1840. Copies of some 5000 sculptures, reliefs and medallions dating back over 5 millennia have been brought together under one roof. Visitors can either buy copies or simply admire the vast collection.

Mon–Fri 09.00–16.00, Wed to 18.00; Sophie-Charlotten-Strasse 17–18; Charlottenburg; S-Bahn station: Westend; Bus: X21, X26, 110, 145

Gothisches Haus (O)

Built around 1500, although much altered in the following centuries, the 'Gothic House' is the oldest house in the city.

Ausstellung zur Baugeschichte Spandaus: Mon–Fri 10.00–17.00, Sat 10.00–13.00; Breite Strasse 32, Spandau; Underground station: Altstadt Spandau

ICC Internationales Congress-Centrum (B–C 4)

This aluminium-fronted structure, 320 m long and 80 m wide, was the combined design of architects Ralf Schüler and Ursulina Schüler-Witte. The building, which looks a bit like a giant spaceship, was erected between 1973 and 1976. The construction costs were the source of great controversy – the final bill came to 1 billion marks. It is the venue for various public events. The huge sculpture at the main entrance is the work of Jean Ipousteguy.

Messedamm, Charlottenburg; Underground station: Kaiserdamm; S-Bahn station: Witzleben; Bus: X21, X49, 104, 149, 204, 219

Kulturforum (F 4)

★ The British architect James Stirling called this complex the 'biggest architectural zoo in the world'. Within a few hundred yards of each other lie the Neue Nationalgalerie (1965–68, Mies van der Rohe), St.-Matthäus-Kirche (1844-46, Stüler), the Philharmonie (1960–63, Scharoun), the Kammermusiksaal (Chamber Music Hall; 1984–87, Wisniewski to plans by Scharoun), the controversial Kunstgewerbemuseum (Museum of Applied Arts; 1973–85, Gutbrod), the Kupferstichkabinett (Collection of Copper Engravings; 1994) and the Gemäldegalerie (Painting Gallery; 1996). Opposite, on Potsdamer Strasse, stands the Staatsbibliothek (National Library; 1967–78 to plans by Scharoun).

Kemperplatz, Tiergarten; Underground station: Potsdamer Platz

Messegelände (B 4–5)

Events such as 'Green Week', the 'International Tourism Exchange', and the biennial 'International Radio Exhibition' attract hundreds of thousands of visitors to this exhibition centre.

Hammarskjöldplatz 1, Charlottenburg; Underground station: Kaiserdamm; S-Bahn station: Witzleben

Olympia-Stadion and Waldbühne (A 4)

The vast Olympic Stadium was built for the 1936 Olympics. Hitler's intention was to use the games as a stage to demonstrate Aryan supremacy. However, the finest athletic performances came from the great black American athlete, Jesse Owens, who won four gold medals. Near the ✪ ⚡ sports complex stands the Waldbühne, an open-air venue resembling a Classical Greek theatre, also built in 1936. It can seat 20000 and is used for concerts which vary from rock to classical. During the summer months, a vast screen is erected to create an open-air cinema.

Am Glockenturm; Charlottenburg; Underground station: Olympia-Stadion; Bus: A18

Reichstag (F 3)

★ Like the Palais des Reichstagspräsidenten opposite, the Reichstag (Parliament Building) was built to plans by Paul Wallot between 1884 and 1894. A tunnel

The World Clock on Alexanderplatz

links the two buildings and was used by Marinus van der Lubbe to enter the Reichstag and set fire to it in 1933. On the day after the fire, under an emergency decree, the basic civil rights guaranteed by the Weimar Constitution were suspended and the death penalty reintroduced. Many historians believe that Hitler engineered the whole episode in order to legitimize his authoritarian powers.

The Reichstag was badly damaged, not just by the fire, but also during World War II. It was restored between 1961 and 1972. In 1990 the first parliamentary session of a reunited Germany was held here. In 1995 the Reichstag was gutted so that the British architect Norman Foster could house the new parliament building within its shell. It will become the permanent seat of the German parliament when the assembly moves here from Bonn in 1999. Other new buildings are under construction to the north and east of the Reichstag.
Platz der Republik, Tiergarten; S-Bahn station: Unter den Linden

Ribbeck-Haus (H 4)
Dating from 1624, this late-Renaissance house with its delicately gabled roof is said to be the only surviving Renaissance house in the city.
Breite Strasse 35, Mitte; Underground station: Spittelmarkt

Riehmers Hofgarten (G 5)
♣ ✿ Constructed at the end of the last century, these buildings are still an impressive example of humane inner-city housing. A master bricklayer by the name of Riehmer built this complex of richly-ornamented five-storey residential blocks between Yorckstrasse, Hagelberger Strasse and Grossbeerenstrasse.
Yorckstrasse 83–86, Kreuzberg; Underground station: Mehringdamm

Rotes Rathaus (H 4)
The Red Town Hall is the headquarters of Berlin City Council, and is not named after a political party, but after the colour of its bricks. Built in neo-Renaissance style between 1861 and 1870, it is encircled by a frieze illustrating the history of Berlin from the 13th to the 19th century.

When the city was partitioned in 1949, the mayor of West Berlin, Ernst Reuter, moved out to Schöneberg Town Hall. After the November Revolution of 1989, it was decided that the reunified city council should return to its original home.
Mon–Fri 09.00–18.00; Rathausstrasse, Mitte; underground and S-Bahn station: Alexanderplatz; Bus: 100, 142, 157, 348

Stasi Headquarters (0)
Normannenstrasse was the headquarters of the GDR's Ministry of State Security (*Staatssicherheit*, hence *Stasi*). Many thousands worked within this high-security complex, which can now be visited by the general public. Exhibits include the office and apartment of Erich Mielke, the notorious minister who oversaw security operations from 1957 to 1989. Other rooms within the museum cover Stasi surveillance techniques, including bugging devices and miniature cameras.
Tues–Fri 11.00–18.00, Sat/Sun 14.00–18.00; entrance Ruschestrasse 103 (Haus 1), Lichtenberg; Underground station: Magdalenenstrasse

Zitadelle Spandau (O)

★ Built on an island in the Havel river, it took about 30 years to erect this Italianate fortress which was completed in 1590. Part of an earlier fortification still stands within its walls: the Juliusturm, dating from the 12th century. The building which now houses the Spandau Heimatmuseum (Local History Museum) also pre-dates the fortress itself, and was probably constructed in around 1220. Along the southern wall you can see gravestones that originally stood in Spandau's Jewish cemetery, destroyed when the Jews were expelled from Mark Brandenburg in 1520.

Tues–Fri 09.00–17.00, Sat/Sun 10.00–17.00, restaurant daily from 11.30; Am Juliusturm, Spandau; Underground station: Zitadelle

PALACES, PARKS & GARDENS

Botanischer Garten (O)

🏃 ❧ Laid out around the turn of the century, the Botanical Gardens boast over 18000 different plant species, and rank among the finest of their kind in the world. At the centre stands a huge glasshouse, where it is easy to pretend you are in a tropical rainforest. One of the most remarkable species on view here is the *victoria amazonica*, a floating plant whose leaves are strong enough to bear the weight of a child (in the Victoria-amazonica-Haus).

Nov–Feb 09.00–16.00, Mar and Oct 09.00–17.00, Apr–Sept 09.00–20.00; museum Tues–Sun 10.00–17.00; Unter den Eichen or Königin-Luise-Strasse entrances, Dahlem; Underground station: Dahlem-Dorf; S-Bahn station: Botanischer Garten; Bus: 183, 101, 148

Glienicker Park, Schloss Klein-Glienicke and Jadgschloss Glienicke (O)

★ One of the finest parks in Berlin. From here it is possible to look across the Havel to Potsdam and Babelsberg, where there are several splendid royal palaces. Before Klein-Glienicke manor house was transformed into a palace, it was the home of minister of state Prince von Hardenberg. In 1816, he instructed P.J. Lenné to lay out a distinctive garden, a project which was continued after Hardenberg's death by the new owner, Prince Carl. But Carl was a great lover of everything Italian and he later asked K.F. Schinkel and his pupils, Persius and von Arnim, to redesign the garden with Italianate features. Wherever you look, an array of Italian-style pavilions, arcades, fountains, gateways and circular benches adorns the view.

On the other side of Königstrasse stands a hunting lodge, built in 1683 for the Great Elector. Over the years, the Jagdschloss has been put to many different uses: from 1712 it was used as a hospital, from 1760 as a carpet factory, and from 1827 as an orphanage. In 1859 F. von Arnim gave the palace its Baroque appearance. When combined with the Babelsberg parks and the Neuer Garten in Potsdam – both landscaped by Lenné – the area constitutes the largest expanse of parkland in Europe.

Königstrasse, Wannsee; S-Bahn station: Wannsee, then bus 116

Jagdschloss Grunewald (O)

This romantic Renaissance palace was built by the Brandenburg elector, Joachim II, in 1542. It was expanded in around 1700 by Martin Grünberg, and given a Baroque exterior at the same time. The rooms are hung with paintings by German and Dutch-Flemish old masters, eg Lucas Cranach the Elder and Peter Paul Rubens. Displayed in the Weapons Store – commissioned by Frederick the Great in 1790 – is an extremely ornate collection of old hunting guns, along with hunting trophies and paintings of hunting scenes.

Mid-May to mid-Oct, Tues–Sun 10.00–13.00, 13.30–17.00, rest of the year only Sat/Sun 10.00–13.00, 13.30–16.00; Am Grunewaldsee, Grunewald; Bus: 115, 183

Pfaueninsel   (O)

★ A mysterious, almost magical, atmosphere surrounds this small island in the Havel river. It has been shrouded in legend ever since the 17th century, when the alchemist Johannes Kunkel tried in vain to make gold here – but instead discovered ruby glass, which became a highly prized commodity. A hundred years later, Friedrich Wilhelm II fell in love with the 76-hectare island when he took a boat trip on the Havel from Potsdam. When he needed to find a hideaway for his mistress, Countess Lichtenau, he decided something special was necessary, something which would completely alter the appearance of the island. So he built a white palace – an inhabitable folly built in the style of a ruined Roman country house – which shone across the water like a theatrical backdrop.

Other similarly romantic buildings followed, such as the Kavaliershaus (1803/24) with its Gothic façade brought from Gdansk, the Schweizerhaus (by Schinkel, 1829–30) and the Fregattenschuppen (by Schadow, 1833). Wilhelm II's love of the sentimental was shared by his successor, Friedrich Wilhelm III, and the latter's wife, Luise. They had a menagerie built, where they kept bears, monkeys, kangaroos, and other exotic animals, such as peacocks (*Pfauen*) which now roam freely around the island – hence the name Pfaueninsel or 'Peacock Island' (previously it had been known by the less exotic name of 'Rabbit Island'). The most attractive part of the island is the landscaped garden with its fountains, ponds, statues and aviary.

Schloss closed in winter; Pfaueninselchaussee, Wannsee; Tel. 805 30 42; bus 116, 216

Schloss Bellevue   (E 3)

Built in 1785 on the edge of the Tiergarten, by Philipp Boumann for August Ferdinand of Prussia, this neo-Classical palace was destroyed in World War II. It was rebuilt during the 1950s, and is now the official Berlin residence of the German president.

Spreeweg, Tiergarten; S-Bahn station: Tiergarten

Schloss Charlottenburg   (C 3)

★ ✿ The Charlottenburg palace garden was laid out about 300 years ago, and is the oldest surviving formal garden in the city. Queen Sophie Charlotte commissioned the Parisian landscape gardener Siméon Godeau to produce a French-style Baroque garden, but his layout was later altered by J.A. Eyserbeck and P.J. Lenné. Beyond the classical French garden, and extending down to the Spree, lies parkland laid out in traditional English style. To the left of the lake stands the mausoleum built by Friedrich Wilhelm III for his wife, Luise, who died thirty years before him. The king, also buried here, is portrayed as much younger than his 70 years.

The palace itself is the combined work of a long line of architects: Nehring (1695–98), Eosander von Göthe (1701–13), Knobelsdorff (1740–46), Langhans (1788–90), and finally Boumann (1790). One of the main attractions inside is the Galerie der Romantik – an extension of the Neue Nationalgalerie – which features an interesting collection of 19th-century paintings by the German Romantics, most notably Caspar David Friedrich.

Some of the historic rooms, including Friedrich II's living quarters, can be viewed as part of a guided tour.
Tues–Fri 09.00–17.00, Sat/Sun 10.00–17.00; Spandauer Damm, Charlottenburg; Underground station: Richard-Wagner-Platz; S-Bahn station: Westend

Tiergarten (E–F 4)
❖ 🏃 The largest and most popular of the city-centre parks was originally woodland, where the aristocracy hunted deer, wild boar, and hare. In the 18th century, under Frederick the Great, the public was allowed access to the grounds, which took a long time to take shape as a park. In 1833 P.J. Lenné started work on the final layout, creating numerous small watercourses, lakes, clearings, meadows, and a 25-km network of footpaths. By the end of World War II, almost all of the original trees had been chopped down for firewood, and much of the resulting open land was used for growing vegetables. Many of the monuments in the park were erected during the 19th century, although the gilded, winged Victory – waving her laurel wreath provocatively towards Paris – at the top of the 67-m Siegessäule (Victory Column) was moved here in 1939 on Hitler's orders.
Strasse des 17. Juni, Tiergarten; Underground station: Hansaplatz; S-Bahn station: Tiergarten

Treptower Park (O)
🏃 A popular destination with plenty of open spaces, centred around the Soviet Memorial to the 22 000 Russian casualties of the Battle of Berlin (1944/45). As well as the monument, fish ponds, busts of Russian and German cosmonauts, and an island in the Spree, the park boasts an observatory dating from 1909, known as the Archenhold Sternwarte.
Guided tours: Wed 18.00, Sat/Sun 15.00; Puschkinallee, Treptow; Tel. 534 80 80; S-Bahn station: Treptower Park

Trümmerberge (Rubble Mountains) (O)
⬍ Berlin suffered untold damage during World War II, more in fact than most other German cities. The huge amounts of rubble that resulted from the bombing raids and the Russian advance had to be disposed of somewhere, so the city fathers decided to make a virtue out of necessity. Between 1946 and 1951, the millions of tons of debris were piled together in the south of Schöneberg district into a 75-m hill. This 'rubble mountain' has since been

grassed over and planted with trees to create a pleasant park, complete with an open-air swimming pool. At the top stands the Wilhelm Foerster Sternwarte (observatory), and at the foot stands the Planetarium (*Munsterdamm, Steglitz; S-Bahn station: Priesterweg*).

Another 'rubble mountain' was created in the Grunewald. Given its position near to the Teufelssee, it was called the Teufelsberg (Devil's Mountain). This heap of bricks and concrete, which reaches a height of 120 m, was not completed until 1968.

Viktoria Park   (G 5)

❖ ✿ In the centre of this park, often referred to as the Kreuzberg ('Mountain of the Cross'), stands Berlin's tallest natural hill, reaching a modest height of 66 m. Until the 18th century, the vineyard on its slopes produced wines which were much appreciated at the royal court. Vines continue to grow in this attractive park, forming what is said to be Germany's northernmost vineyard. During the Napoleonic Wars, the Kreuzberg performed an important strategic function: in 1813 a system of trenches was dug to defend the city against Napoleon's troops.
Kreuzbergstrasse, Kreuzberg; Underground station: Mehringdamm

Zoos

❖ ✿ As a result of decades of partition, Berlin now boasts two zoos. The city's original zoo (**E4**), which dates from 1841 and was the first zoo in Germany, is situated in a central location in the western part of the city. Only 91 of the 4000 creatures (1400 species of mammals and birds in all) survived World War II. Since then the Zoologischer Garten has expanded rapidly, and now boasts 11 000 animals, and more species than any other in the world. Probably the most famous inhabitant is the Chinese panda known as Bao-Bao. The zoo authorities are particularly proud of the aquarium, in a building which also houses an insectarium and a terrarium.
Daily 09.00–18.30, winter to 17.00; Budapesterstrasse, Charlottenburg; Tel. 25 40 12 55; Underground and S-Bahn station: Zoologischer Garten

The second zoo, the Tierpark, (**0**) was established in the grounds of the Baroque palace in Friedrichsfelde, and today is home to some 5000 animals (900 different species). The zoo has more than 50 enclosures and animal houses. After years of restoration work, the palace (1690) is now open to the public.
Daily 09.00–19.00, winter Tues–Sun 09.00–16.30; palace: Tues–Fri 10.00–18.00, Sat 10.00–16.00, Sun 13.00–18.00; Strasse am Tierpark, Lichtenberg; Tel. 51 53 10; Underground station: Tierpark; S-Bahn station: Friedrichsfelde

SQUARES

Alexanderplatz   (H 3)

❖ The 'Alex', as this square is popularly known, was once a parade ground. It was named after the Russian tsar in 1805, but was not to achieve international fame until 1929, when Alfred Döblin's celebrated novel *Berlin Alexanderplatz* was published. During the 1960s, the GDR government enlarged the square, surrounding it with drab, box-like architecture, with the aim of turning it into a showpiece for their socialist metropolis. This windswept expanse of concrete was the scene of tumultuous events during the final days of the GDR: a million people gathered here on 4 November 1989 to demand the right to assemble, to demonstrate, and to read a free press. A further revamp is planned for this bleak open space, which will probably reflect modern American city style.

On the other side of the S-Bahn stands the 365-m Fernsehturm (TV tower), at the top of which the Tele-Café rotates on its axis once every hour. Although originally derided by Westerners as an eyesore, the Fernsehturm has survived the GDR regime and is now a popular tourist attraction. The view, extending for 40 km on a clear day, is tremendous, and so an ascent is definitely worth queueing for.
Mitte; underground and S-Bahn station: Alexanderplatz

Gendarmenmarkt (G 4)

★ This square was known as the Gendarmenmarkt until 1950, when its name was changed to Platz der Akademie. After reunification Berliners readopted its original name, the origins of which can be traced back to the 18th century, when the stables of the Gens d'Armes Regiment surrounded the Deutscher Dom and the Französischer Dom on this site. Both of these cathedrals were built between 1701 and 1708, with Carl von Gontard adding domes about 80 years later, as Frederick the Great wanted to recreate the splendour of Rome's Piazza del Populo. Both churches are richly adorned with sculptures.

The Französischer Dom (French Cathedral) at the northern end of the square is now, appropriately, the home of the Huguenot Museum – the church was, after all, originally built for the 20 000 French emigrants living in exile in Prussia. There is a good view of the surrounding area from the small wine bar in the tower, but there are 80 steps to climb. Between the two cathedrals stands Schinkel's impressive, neo-Classical Schauspielhaus (Playhouse, 1818–21). Gutted during 1943, it was finally reopened in 1984 and is now home to the Berlin Symphony Orchestra; and so, strictly speaking, is a concert hall, not a playhouse. At Christmas 1989, Leonard Bernstein conducted a performance of Beethoven's *Ninth Symphony* here to celebrate the political transformation of the previous month. A marble statue of the famous playwright, Friedrich Schiller (1759–1805) – many of whose plays were concerned with freedom in all its forms – stands outside the Schauspielhaus.
Mitte: Underground station: Stadtmitte

Lustgarten/Schlossplatz (G 3)

Known as Marx-Engels-Platz until 1994, Schlossplatz is not a congenial place to sit and relax. This important focal point in front of what used to be the Schloss (Palace) is now surrounded by a series of monolithic structures built during the communist era. To the communists, the Schloss was a symbol of Germany's recent imperial past. Although it had been badly damaged during the war, it was not beyond repair, but in 1950 the GDR government ordered the ruined building to be blown up. The space it occupied was filled in 1976 by the Palast der Republik, a vast entertainments complex with restaurants, cafés, a theatre and bowling alley, but shortly before reunification, asbestos was discovered in the fabric of the building and it was closed. Currently just a shell, its future is uncertain. Reflected in its copper-coloured façade is the Berliner Dom (Berlin Cathedral), which was built by Raschdorff between 1893 and 1905. In the Lustgarten, once a pleasure garden commissioned by the Great Elector, stands the Altes Museum (built by Schinkel, 1823–29). This imposing neo-Classical building with its arcaded porch has just reopened after renovation, and houses antiquities relocated from Charlottenburg. In front of the building is a granite bowl of huge dimensions: 7 m in diameter, and weighing 76 tonnes. The idea was Schinkel's, but it was the master mason Cantian who had the awesome task of carving this huge bowl from an Ice Age boulder (1834).

At the southern end of Schlossplatz stands the late GDR's Staatsrat (State Council). Although it shows some distinctively Stalinist architectural features, its appearance is enhanced by the inclusion in its façade of a portal from the Schloss. It was from this very spot that the GDR's hero Karl Liebknecht proclaimed a socialist republic on 9 November 1918.

Opposite stands the neo-Baroque Neuer Marstall (New Stables, 1896–1902), where royal coaches and horses were kept for ceremonial events. It is now used as a library and exhibition space,

and houses the Academy of Arts. Nearby in Breite Strasse stand the Alter Marstall ('Old Stables') and the Ribbeck-Haus (1624).

Mitte; S-Bahn station: Hackescher Markt

Potsdamer Platz/Info Box (F–G 4)

⚡ Once the busiest square in Europe, after the war it became a derelict wasteland in the shadow of the Berlin Wall. Now Europe's largest building site, it is being converted into a major commercial district with Daimler-Benz, Sony, and other multinational companies set to establish their German head offices here. As well as offices, there will be hotels, entertainment complexes and restaurants, but very little residential accommodation. An idea of how it will look in the future can be gleaned from models, films, computer simulations and lots of other hi-tech gadgetry in the giant, red Info Box.

Info Box open until 31 Dec 2000, daily 09.00–19.00, Thurs to 21.00; Groups and guided tours, call 22 55 24-0; Leipziger Platz 21, Mitte; Underground and S-Bahn station: Potsdamer Platz; Bus: 142, 248, 348

The Elefantentor – entrance to the Zoologischer Garten

A tour round the museums

Berlin's two sets of museums are undergoing a reunification process of their own

As with so many public services in Berlin today, the city's museums east and west of the old divide are going through a period of upheaval. Ever since the collapse of the Wall, archivists and curators have been arguing about what is the best way to bring groups of exhibits back together, and how the limited resources available can be used most wisely. Thankfully, only a small proportion of Berlin's artistic and historic treasures were destroyed during the war, but it means the curators have a Herculean task on their hands.

Many of the museums began life in the early 19th century, when Wilhelm II wanted to establish somewhere to house his collection of royal treasures. Initially he commissioned Schinkel to design a suitable building, but when German archaeologists, notably Carl Richard Lepsius and Heinrich Schliemann, began plundering the sites of Egypt and

The Pergamon Altar is the centrepiece of Berlin's collection of antiquities

Asia Minor, more room was required to house the booty.

At the start of World War II, most of the historic collections were carefully stored away, in mine shafts or other such safe places. Most were returned to Berlin after the war, and whether exhibits found their way to East or West Berlin depended on where they had been hidden. As a result of the city's partition, coherent collections were split down the middle, and the authorities in East and West made little attempt to cooperate with one another. Paintings by Berlin artists, Adolph von Menzel, for example, were divided up between the Alte Nationalgalerie in East Berlin which houses *The Iron Foundry*, and the Neue National Galerie in West Berlin which owns *The Flute Player*. Botticelli's illustrations of Dante's *Divine Comedy* were likewise divided; *Hell* found its way to the West, *Paradise* to the East.

In West Berlin, the great state museums were amalgamated under the Stiftung Preussischer Kulturbesitz (Prussian Cultural Heritage Foundation), with the main exhibition centres in Dahlem

(Ethnographic Museum, Islamic, Indian and East Asian Art), around the Kulturforum complex at the Tiergarten (New National Gallery, Museum of Applied Art, Picture Gallery, Collection of Copper Engravings), and in Charlottenburg (Egyptian Museum, Ancient and Early History Museum). Now that the city has been reunited, these museums have been joined by those on the Museumsinsel (Museum Island), such as Schinkel's Altes Museum (1830), the Neues Museum, the Alte Nationalgalerie, the Bode-Museum and the Pergamon-Museum. The cost of rebuilding the Neues Museum and renovating the Bode-Museum is estimated at 1.2 billion marks, and the new buildings in the Kulturforum cost almost the same. Now, at last, the authorities are working together. Clearly the Museumsinsel has a high priority, particularly as the buildings themselves are of great architectural interest and variety. Schinkel, Stüler, Strack, Ihne, Hoffmann, and Messel are among the prominent architects who designed them.

At least one thing has now been firmly established: the archaeological collections will be concentrated on the Museumsinsel, once the Neues Museum has been restored, so Nefertiti will have to move from her present home in Charlottenburg. The anthropological and non-European collections will be concentrated in Dahlem, while the European collections will be kept at the Kulturforum, the Bode-Museum and the Alte Nationalgalerie.

There are many museums in Dahlem, Charlottenburg, and Tiergarten which are not part of the Stiftung Preussischer Kulturbesitz, but which should not be overlooked by the visitor. The Bröhan-Museum, for example, keeps a private collection of Jugendstil and Art Deco ceramics and furniture; the high point of the Museum für Naturkunde (Natural History Museum) in Invalidenstrasse is the brachiosaurus skeleton; while the Deutsches Technikmuseum (Technology Museum) in Kreuzberg has developed into a major attraction within the space of a few years. In addition, there are many smaller, specialist museums – in fact, there are no less than 180 museums in Berlin, not including the many touring exhibitions.

Entrance to the museums of the Stiftung Preussischer Kulturbesitz is free on the first Sunday in the month (though not for the temporary exhibitions).

Ägyptisches Museum (C 4)

★ ‡ The *Bust of Queen Nefertiti*, said to be the most beautiful in history, has been kept here in the Egyptian Museum since 1920. Excavated in Akhetaten in Egypt in 1912 by Ludwig Borchardt, it was the creation of an unknown sculptor in 1340 BC. It is the museum's most prized exhibit, and one which, over the years, has entranced millions of visitors. *Queen Teja* is captivating in a different way. This tiny head (1360 BC), carved from yew wood, is only 9.5 cm tall, but perfectly worked. Other treasures housed here include the Kalabsha Monumental Gate, a colonnaded courtyard from King Sahu-Re's Temple of the Dead, death masks, papyri, jewellery and toys.

Tues–Fri 09.00–17.00, Sat/Sun 10.00–17.00; Schlossstrasse 70, Charlottenburg; Bus: X21, X26, 109, 110, 145

Bauhaus-Archiv
Museum für Gestaltung (E–F 5)
The building that houses the Design Museum is the work of Walter Gropius, who founded the influential Bauhaus school of design, crafts and architecture in Weimar in 1919. The school moved to Dessau in 1925, and then on to Berlin, only to be closed by the Nazis in 1933. Works representing the full scope of Bauhaus activities are displayed here: architectural models by Gropius, Meyer, van der Rohe; furniture by Breuer; paintings by Kandinsky, Klee, and Feininger; metalwork and ceramics.
Wed–Mon 10.00–17.00; Klingelhöferstrasse 14, Tiergarten; Underground station: Nollendorfplatz; Bus: 100, 129, 187, 341

Berlin-Museum (G 5)
★ 🚸 The famous judge and writer E.T.A. Hoffmann used to hear legal cases in the old Court of Appeal (built in the 1730s). Beautifully restored, the building now houses exhibits documenting the city's history, such as maps, plans, models, paintings, sculpture, *objets d'art*, as well as

MARCO POLO SELECTION: MUSEUMS

1 **Ägyptisches Museum**
Nefertiti, reckoned to be 3330 years old, is still the most beautiful face in Berlin (page 38)

2 **Technisches Museum**
A 'hands-on' museum which will fascinate technically-minded children and teenagers (page 40)

3 **Berlin-Museum**
Currently closed, but both the old building and Libeskind's new building are fascinating to see (page 39)

4 **Bröhan-Museum**
Jugendstil and art deco, furniture, ceramics, glassware and *objets d'art* (page 40)

5 **Haus am Checkpoint Charlie**
A home-made aircraft is just one exhibit demonstrating the inventiveness of GDR escapees (page 41)

6 **Sammlung Berggruen**
Works by Picasso and other contemporaries – a real gem (page 42)

7 **Märkisches Museum**
Mechanical instruments and music boxes tinkle old-fashioned parlour tunes (page 41)

8 **Museum für Naturkunde**
Marvel at the 12-m high skeleton of the famous *brachiosaurus brancai* (page 42)

9 **Museum für Völkerkunde**
The South Sea Islanders' boats are imaginatively presented and accessible to children (page 44)

10 **Pergamon-Museum**
Dedicated to the goddess Athena, the Pergamon Altar with its beautiful frieze never fails to captivate (page 45)

fashions, furniture and toys from the 16th century to the present day. It is closed until 1999, awaiting the completion of a major extension that will hold all of the Jewish Museum.

Lindenstrasse 14, Kreuzberg; Underground station: Hallesches Tor

Bröhan-Museum (C 4)

★ Anyone who likes Jugendstil and Art Deco will be enthralled by Karl Bröhan's collection. It includes a wide range of furniture, paintings from the *Berliner Sezession* movement, porcelain, glass and ceramics. Prized exhibits include Emile Gallé's vases, furniture by Hector Guimard and Louis Majorelle, metalwork by Henry van de Velde and a collection of Bohemian glass.

Tues–Sun 10.00–18.00; Schlossstrasse 1a, Charlottenburg; Underground station: Sophie-Charlotte-Platz; Bus: X21, X26, 109, 110, 145

Brücke-Museum (O)

Situated on the edge of the Grunewald, a visit to this museum can easily be combined with a woodland walk. On display are works of art by the group known as *Die Brücke* ('The Bridge'). This movement, founded in Dresden in 1905, was led by Karl Schmidt-Rottluff, a leading light in German Expressionism. He and his acolytes, such as Kirchner, Nolde and Pechstein, sought to 'bridge' the gap between figurative and abstract art.

Wed–Mon 11.00–17.00; Bussardsteig 9, Dahlem; bus 115

Deutsches Historisches Museum (G 4)

The Museum of German History is situated in the Baroque Zeughaus and houses the German historical collections, temporary exhibitions and a cinema.

Thurs–Tues 10.00–18.00; Unter den Linden 2, Mitte; Bus: 100, 157, 348

Deutsches Technisches Museum (F–G 5)

★ ✳ This, the Museum of Technology, is one of Berlin's newest museums and is very popular with children. The main section has a huge collection of bicycles, as well as other forms of transport such as cars, steam locomotives, model ships, hot-air balloons and aircraft. Many of the displays are hands-on and there is even an experiment room where children can play with computers and various hi-tech gadgets.

Tues–Fri 09.00–17.30, Sat/Sun 10.00–18.00; Trebbiner Strasse 9 and Möckernstrasse 26, Kreuzberg; Tel. 25 48 41 24; Underground station: Möckernbrücke; S-Bahn station: Gleisdreieck

Gedenkstätte Deutscher Widerstand (F 5)

This 19th-century building is now a German Resistance Memorial, but between 1918 and 1935, it was the Ministry of Defence headquarters, and from then until the end of the war the Supreme Army Command. It was here on 20 July 1944 that Graf Schenk von Stauffenberg and a number of other senior army officers made an unsuccessful attempt on Hitler's life. They were all court-martialled and summarily shot. The building is now a permanent memorial to those Germans who fought National Socialism from within.

Mon–Fri 09.00–18.00, Sat/Sun 09.00–13.00; Stauffenbergstrasse

13–14, Tiergarten; Underground station: Kurfürstenstrasse

Gedenkstätte Haus der Wannseekonferenz (O)

It was in this villa beside the Wannsee that representatives of the SS and the Nazi government met in January 1942 to reach a decision on what should be done with the Jews, a decision often chillingly described as the 'final solution' to the 'Jewish question'. The decision that was reached and then ruthlessly implemented was that the 10 million Jews in France, Poland and Russia should be exterminated. Inside the villa is an exhibition showing how the planned genocide was carried out: from segregation and persecution to deportation and eventual murder.

Tues–Fri 10.00–18.00, Sat/Sun 14.00–18.00; Am Grossen Wannsee 56–58, Zehlendorf; S-Bahn station: Wannsee, then bus: 114

Gedänkstätte Plötzensee (D 2)

This memorial commemorates the prison where dissidents and political opponents were brought for imprisonment and execution during the Nazi regime. Altogether some 2500 innocent people were murdered here.

Daily 08.30–18.00 (Mar–Sept), 08.30–16.30 (Oct–Feb); Hüttigpfad, Charlottenburg; S-Bahn station: Beusselstrasse (under construction); Bus: 123, 126

Hamburger Bahnhof (F 3)

Built in 1846/47, this former railway station has been restored as an exhibition centre for the contemporary collection of the Nationalgalerie: Beuys, Warhol, Lichtenstein, Kienholz, Baselitz,

and others are represented here.

Tues–Fri 09.00–17.00, Sat/Sun 10.00–17.00; Invalidenstrasse 50/51, Tiergarten; S-Bahn station: Lehrter Stadtbahnhof; bus 219, 245, 248

Haus am Checkpoint Charlie (Berlin Wall Museum) (G 4)

★ ✝ Founded after the construction of the Wall on 13 August 1961, this museum looks beyond the physical reality of the Wall during the 29 years of its existence. It documents life and death associated with the Wall, by retelling the dramatic stories of those who tried, successfully or tragically, to cross the border.

Daily 09.00–22.00; Friedrichstrasse 44, Kreuzberg; Underground station: Kochstrasse; Bus: 129

Jüdisches Museum (G 4)

The collections documenting the history of Berlin's Jewish community are currently being re-organized. The new Jewish Museum, designed by the architect Daniel Libeskind, resembles a stone streak of lightning. Nearing completion, it will form an extension to the Berlin-Museum.

Stresemannstrasse 110, Kreuzberg; Underground station: Potsdamer Platz; S-Bahn station: Anhalter Bahnhof; Bus: 129, 248, 341

Märkisches Museum (H 4)

★ ✝ This museum covers the history of Berlin and Brandenburg. Standing beside the river Spree, it looks remarkably like a cathedral. The architect L. Hoffmann, who worked on the project from 1901–1907, produced a rather strange blend of architectural styles. The oldest exhibit here is a 7th-millennium BC deer mask, the earliest evidence of human habitation in the region. The collection of mechanical and musical instruments always attracts interest. Another section of the museum deals with the contemporary history of Berlin, with a particular focus on the dramatic events leading to the fall of the Wall in November 1989.

Tues–Sun 10.00–18.00; Am Köllnischen Park 5, Mitte; Underground station: Märkisches Museum

Museum für Naturkunde (G 3)

★ ‡ In its 280-year history, the Natural History Museum has acquired hundreds of thousands of artefacts, but obviously there is not enough room to show them all. Among the most memorable exhibits in the 16-room display are the dinosaur skeletons from East Africa, the most famous of which is the *brachiosaurus brancai*. At 12 m tall and 23 m long, it is reckoned to be the largest reconstructed skeleton in the world. Not far away are the fossilized remains of the prehistoric bird *archaeopteryx lithographica*.

Tues–Sun 09.30–17.00; Invalidenstrasse 43, Mitte; Underground station: Zinnowitzer Strasse; Bus: 157, 245, 340

Museumsdorf Düppel (O)

‡ A reconstruction of the medieval Brandenburg village that stood on this site around 1200. The fields and gardens have been planted with the original crops and wild flowers, and the old fruit varieties are cultivated. Sheep, goats, pigs, an ox, and many different kinds of poultry wander around the village. Demonstrations of ancient crafts such as weaving, pottery, and construction techniques are given.

Thurs 15.00–19.00, Sun and public holidays 10.00–17.00 (Apr–Oct); Clauertstrasse 11, Zehlendorf; Bus: 115, 129, 211

Sammlung Berggruen (C 3/4)

★ Art dealer Heinz Berggruen has loaned his marvellous collection of paintings by Picasso, Klee, and their contemporaries to the people of Berlin for 10 years. You can see them in the Stüler-Bau opposite Schloss Charlottenburg.

Tues–Fri 09.00–17.00, Sat/Sun 10.00–17.00; Schlossstrasse 70, Charlottenburg; Underground station: Sophie-Charlotte-Platz; Bus: X21, X26, 109, 110, 145

Topographie des Terrors (G 4)

It was on this site, covering a total of 62 000 sq m, that the Gestapo, SS, and Reich security officials planned their reign of terror against the Jewish people and opponents of the Nazis. This was the command centre for the SS units in the occupied territories. Scattered around the derelict site are boards pointing out the locations of all the various institutions whose staff were dedicated to wiping out the Jews. Between 1939 and 1945 many resistance fighters and other opponents of the Nazis were imprisoned and tortured here.

All the buildings in the complex were destroyed after the war, and the wasteland they once occupied is awaiting redevelopment. There are plans for a permanent monument to the victims of the Gestapo, with a study centre and museum. In a temporary exhibition hall, and in the cellars of the adjoining building, which used to be the Gestapo headquarters at 8, Prinz-Albrecht-Strasse (now Niederkirchnerstrasse), visitors can learn about the command structure of the SS.

Daily 10.00–18.00, Stresemannstrasse 110 (next to Martin-Gropius-Bau), Kreuzberg; Underground station: Kochstrasse; S-Bahn station: Anhalter Bahnhof or Potsdamer Platz

KULTURFORUM MUSEUMS

Gemäldegalerie (F 4)

The Picture Gallery started out as the Elector's private art collection. Today it comprises: German, Dutch and Italian works of art from the 13th to the 16th century; Dutch and Flemish Baroque; English, French, Italian and Spanish works from the 17th and 18th centuries. Among the 600 works on show are pictures by Dürer, Cranach, Holbein, Brueghel, Titian, Rubens, Rembrandt, Canaletto, Velázquez and Watteau, to name but a few of the most famous masters. Previously housed in Dahlem, the gallery now resides in brand new, purpose-built premises in the Kulturforum.

Kunstgewerbemuseum (F 5)

Rolf Gutbrod's design for the Museum of Applied Arts aroused considerable controversy: many critics felt that it did not fit in well with the other buildings in the Kulturforum complex. But then it does have room for every conceivable kind of applied art, including gold and silver work, glassware, majolica, jewellery, porcelain, furniture and clothing. The most prized exhibits are mostly treasures assembled from churches and abbeys all over Germany, but the museum's highlight is the magnificent Renaissance silverware from Lüneberg Town Hall. The Jugendstil section is very interesting, as is the design department, where the exhibits are predominantly tableware and household items from Bauhaus to the 1980s.

Kupferstichkabinett (F 4)

The Great Elector laid the foundations for this important collection of prints, drawings and engravings. The original collection of 2500 drawings for the Brandenburg-Prussian Court Library has grown to 25000 drawings and 380000 prints, dating from the Middle Ages to the present day.

Musikinstrumenten-Museum (F 4)

♪ This extraordinarily comprehensive collection of European musical instruments and music-related historical documents is kept in a modern building (1984) between the Philharmonie and the Kammermusiksaal. Among the fine old instruments on display are flutes which belonged to the Prussian king, Friedrich II, Sophie Charlotte of Prussia's portable harpsichord, and some priceless violins. At the heart of the building is a large Wurlitzer organ (1929), which is played every Saturday at 12.00.

Neue Nationalgalerie (F 4)

Like almost every other museum collection in Berlin, the 19th- and 20th-century paintings and sculptures were split between the two halves of the city after World War II. In the 1960s, West Berlin's art critics warmly welcomed Bauhaus architect Mies van der Rohe's custom-built premises for the New National Gallery on the edge of the Tiergarten. The works displayed here are principally by 20th-century artists, although later works by 19th-century artists Liebermann, Corinth and Slevogt are also included in the collection. Leading names include Beckmann, Munch, Hodler, Kokoschka, Klee and Feininger, plus many artists of the 'Brücke' group, Dadaists, Surrealists, Cubists, Fauvists and exponents of the *Neue Sachlichkeit* ('New Objectivity') movement.

All Kulturforum museums: Tues–Fri 09.00–17.00, Sat/Sun 10.00–17.00; Matthäikirchplatz 8, Tiergarten; underground and S-Bahn station: Potsdamer Platz; bus 142, 148, 248, 348

DAHLEM MUSEUMS

(0) The three-storey museum building in Berlin's quiet and leafy suburb of Dahlem was constructed between 1912 and 1971. It houses several different museums. Note that the Gemäldegalerie (Picture Gallery) has now been transferred to the Kulturforum complex.

Museum für Völkerkunde

★ ‡ Here, in the Ethnographic Museum, the cultural histories of American, Asian, African, Australian and non-German-speaking European peoples is documented through a huge variety of exhibits. Of special interest are the boats and dwellings of the South Sea Islanders – these are imaginatively presented and very child-friendly. Other interesting exhibits are the masks and sculptures from Africa, and the priceless sacred objects of the Nazca and Mayan civilizations. The museum is scheduled to be restored and extended from the year 2000.

Museum für Indische Kunst

The Indian Art Museum has its origins in a collection separated from the Museum für Völkerkunde in 1963 and enlarged. Mainly art from India, Nepal and Tibet as well as stone sculptures, plaster and bronze images of deities, plus some unique wall paintings from Turkestan, known as the Turfan-Sammlung.

The Neue Nationalgalerie – designed by Mies van der Rohe

Closed for two years from mid-1998 for restoration

Museum für Islamische Kunst

At the entrance a huge Persian garden carpet, dating from the 18th century, forms a perfect introduction to this beautiful collection of Islamic Art. Other treasures in the museum include a 400-year-old prayer niche and a wooden dome from the Alhambra in Granada.

Museum für Ostasiatische Kunst

The Museum of East Asian Art contains paintings, prints, bronzes and various *objets d'art* from China, Japan and Korea. It remains a rather small collection, as many fine exhibits were lost in World War II, and it is becoming increasingly difficult to acquire new permanent exhibits from this part of the world.

Closed for a two-year-period of restoration from mid-1998

All Dahlem museums: Tues–Fri 09.00–17.00, Sat/Sun 10.00–17.00; Lansstrasse 8, Dahlem; Underground station: Dahlem Dorf

MUSEUMSINSEL

Altes Museum   (G 3)

Like so many of its other priceless collections, Berlin's collection of antiquities was split up after the war. Some exhibits were displayed in Charlottenburg in West Berlin, some on the Museumsinsel in East Berlin. Now the Charlottenburg collection, including such prized exhibits as the Hildesheim Silver Treasure, has been moved to the newly renovated Altes Museum.

Entrance: Lustgarten

Bode-Museum   (G 3)

Currently sharing Berlin's Egyptian collection with the Ägyptisches Museum in Charlottenburg, the Bode-Museum will close in August 1998 for restoration. When it reopens, it will house not only the Ägyptisches Museum, but also the sculpture collection alongside late-Classical and Byzantine art.

Entrance: Monbijoubrücke

Pergamon-Museum   (G 3)

★ ☘ This museum, arguably Berlin's most prestigious, opened in 1930. It was named after the reconstructed Pergamon Altar, a masterpiece of Hellenistic architecture, dating from 180–159 BC and unearthed near Bergama in western Turkey by archaeologist Carl Humann, who shipped it to Berlin in 1903. Also within the complex is the Museum für Islamische Kunst (Museum for Islamic Art; not to be confused with its counterpart in Dahlem), where the prized exhibit is the decorated façade of the desert palace of Mschatta. The Near Eastern Museum houses the enormous blue Ishtar Gate and the Processional Way from Babylon.

Entrance: Am Kupfergraben

All museums on the Museumsinsel: Daily (except Mon) 09.00-17.00; Am Kupfergraben, Mitte; Underground and S-Bahn station: Friedrichstrasse; Bus: 100, 157, 348

The Museumsinsel is also home to the Neues Museum, under reconstruction, and the Alte Nationalgalerie, which will reopen in 2001 after major rebuilding work is complete, and will house 19th-century paintings and sculptures.

Cosmopolitan cuisine

Berlin is famous for its bar culture – Berliners are as happy to dine in a traditional Kneipe as in an exotic restaurant

From the *Ratskeller* of the Great Elector's day and the billiard halls of Frederick the Great's era to Lutter & Wegener's wine bars and *Café Grössenwahn* – since time immemorial, Berliners have gathered together to eat and drink and set the world to rights. Berlin's bar and café culture has a long tradition, and many of the old names have survived the political upheavals, including *Café Kranzler, Kempinski* and *Café Bauer,* to name but three of the most famous.

But there have been new developments over the years. The city's green areas now boast a wide selection of *Gartenlokale* or *Ausflugslokale* – country cafés or restaurants with outdoor seating, often along the shores of the lakes. However, seasonal fluctuations in demand, and dependence on the weather do not bring out the best in the catering trade, so you may prefer to make do with a cup of tea and a ham roll, and get a proper meal back in town

Berlin's restaurants testify to the city's cosmopolitan culture

later on. You will be spoilt for choice in the city centre. In some areas, between Bleibtreustrasse and Savignyplatz for example, the choice is overwhelming. Other areas where eateries proliferate include Kreuzberg, Prenzlauer Berg, and Schöneberg.

As in many other major cities, you can sample food from all over the world: from France, Spain, Russia, Turkey, the Middle East, China, Indonesia – the list could go on and on. However, Berlin is a truly multicultural city, and Italians, Turks, and Greeks make up a significant part of the population. They have brought their culinary skills along with them – and have found a ready market. The Italians have probably the highest profile. With about 600 restaurants, they represent a large share of Berlin's gastronomic market. And justifiably so: in most of these establishments, the ambience is more than agreeable and the food is good and reasonably priced. In the *Ponte Vecchio, Don Camillo* or *Bacco* for example, Italian chefs have produced something out of the ordinary. *Bar Centrale* on Yorckstrasse must

MARCO POLO SELECTION: RESTAURANTS

1 Bar Centrale
Upmarket bistro in the fashionable *New York* cinema (page 50)

2 Borchardt
A chic restaurant where you can dine in style (page 55)

3 Grand Slam
Johannes King serves some gastronomic aces near the Dahlem tennis courts (page 51)

4 Merhaba
Top class Turkish restaurant without the exotic trappings (page 56)

5 Ponte Vecchio
A classy Italian restaurant, not too expensive (page 54)

6 Restauration 1900
A fashionable place to dine out in Prenzlauer Berg. Mainly German fare, but with a few surprises (page 52)

7 Maxwell
Fine meals and great atmosphere – in a former brewery (page 56)

8 Trio
Excellent food at reasonable prices (page 55)

9 Oren
Jewish, vegetarian, and always packed (page 57)

10 Café im Literaturhaus
Great atmosphere in one of the Ku'damm's smartest side streets (page 53)

be one of the city's most popular Italian bar-restaurants. Even some of the basic pizzerias provide very palatable fare. In Kreuzberg, the district often described as 'Little Istanbul', Turkish restaurants and snack bars abound, particularly in the Kottbusser Tor and Schlesisches Tor areas, although by far the best is the *Merhaba* at Hasenheide 39.

But if it is traditional Berlin fare that you are looking for, then you may have to look a little harder. Bear in mind that 'real' Berlin cooking is quite heavy and also French-influenced – by which we mean not *haute cuisine*, but the everyday food of the Huguenots. If you go to where real Berlin food is prepared, to *Hardtke*, to the more basic *Grossbeerenkeller* or to the *Nussbaum*, you will find some hearty special-

ities on the menu. Typical dishes include: *Eisbein mit Erbsenpüree* (knuckle of pork with pease pudding), *Rinderroulade* (beef olives) or *Kohlroulade* (cabbage roll), *Wildragout* (game stew), *Hühnerfrikassee* (fricassee of chicken), *Bouletten* with *Griebenschmalz* (meatballs with dripping), finished off with a *Kompott* (stewed fruit), plus some other traditional Teutonic specialities such as *Löffelerbsen Berliner Art* (thick soup with peas, pig's ears, trotters and tails) and *Berliner Schlachtplatte* (fresh blood and liver sausage, pig's kidney and boiled pork).

Snack bars and roadside stalls (*Imbiss*) selling tasty *Bratwurst* sausages and chips are a common sight everywhere in Germany, but the most popular snack in Berlin is the *Currywurst*, a fried sausage drenched in curry sauce.

Turkish and Greek snack bars selling kebabs and gyros in a pitta are taking an increasing share of the market. All the usual fast-food outlets and burger bars are to be found in the central area.

By law, all restaurants must display their menu and prices by the door. They also have to state their opening times, including their *Ruhetag* or closing day.

AUSFLUGSLOKALE

No Berliner's weekend is complete without a walk in the woods, followed by a drink or something more substantial in one of the many *Ausflugslokale*.
T = terrace

Alter Dorfkrug Lübars (T) (O)
Lübars is the last proper village within Berlin's city limits. The 'Old Village Inn' boasts a large and popular beer garden. Now that Berliners have more places to choose from, competition has led to a vast improvement in the quality of food served here.
Wed–Sun 11.30–22.00; Alt-Lübars 8, Lübars; Tel. 402 71 74; Bus: 222

Blockhaus Nikolskoe (T) (O)
↯ Situated in secluded woodland, this Russian-style *dacha* was a gift from Friedrich Wilhelm III to his daughter and her fiancé, the future Tsar Nicholas I of Russia, in 1818. The lovely view across the Havel is adequate compensation for the mediocre food and rather grumpy service. Very popular despite its drawbacks, so you should either arrive early or book a table in advance.
Fri–Wed 10.00–22.00 (winter to 20.00); Nikolskoer Weg 15, Wannsee; Tel. 805 29 14; Bus: 216

Brauhaus in Rixdorf (T) (O)
Fin-de-siècle industrialist's villa, whose attractions include a large garden and home-brewed beer. Definitely worth the journey.
Daily 11.30–01.00, Fri/Sat to 03.00; Glasower Strasse 27, Neukölln; Tel. 626 88 80; Underground station: Grenzallee, Hermannstrasse; S-Bahn station: Hermannstrasse

Chalet Suisse (T) (O)
Swiss specialities such as *raclette* (a melted cheese dish), *Bündnerfleisch* (cured beef) and *rösti* (potato pancakes with various toppings). Asparagus, salmon, mushrooms etc. are served when in season. In the Grunewald, but not too remote, with pond, animal corner and a good children's playground, so that weary parents can savour their glass of Dôle du Valais in peace.
Daily 11.30–24.00; Im Jagen 5, Grunewald; Tel. 832 63 62; Bus: 115

Hotel Müggelsee (T) (O)
❧ Largest *Ausflugslokal* in the east of the city, plus hotel. By the Müggelsee. Good starting point for circular walks, cycle tours and boat cruises.
Daily 11.30–23.00, Am Grossen Müggelsee, Köpenick; Tel. 658 82-0; Bus: 169

Remise (T) (O)
In Schloss Klein-Glienicke, situated in the wonderful surroundings of Glienicke Park. Friendly service, excellent food and substantial prices.
Wed–Sun from 12.00; Königstrasse, Wannsee; Tel. 805 40 00; Bus 116

Söhnelhof (T) (O)
Next to a boatyard located on the Teltowkanal. In the summer, diners can sit out on the spacious

terrace; in the winter, they can sit inside the warm, cosy cottage. Whatever the season, you can enjoy traditional German fare which is well above average for an *Ausflugslokal*.

Wed–Sat 12.00–22.00, Sun 12.00–21.00; Neue Kreisstrasse 50, Wannsee; Tel. 805 20 72; Bus: 118

Strandbaude (T) (O)

❀❧ Unprepossessing exterior, usually (but not always) compensated for by good food: often game dishes and locally-caught fish. Fishing and rowing nearby, ice-skating in the winter. The old East-West border used to cross the Gross Glienicke See, said to be Berlin's cleanest lake.

Wed–Sun 11.00–22.00, winter to 21.00; Verlängerte Uferpromenade, Kladow; Tel. 365 44 62; Bus: 134, 135

BARS & KNEIPEN

Bar am Lützowplatz (E–F 4)

The best thing about this place is the counter, as endless as the bar itself; the second-best thing is the late-night crowds that drop in for a nightcap on their way home.

Daily 15.00–05.00; Lützowplatz 7, Schöneberg; Tel. 262 68 07; Underground station: Nollendorfplatz

Bar Centrale (G 5)

★ ⚕ This trendy bar is almost always full, especially when the film at the cinema next door has just ended. Popular with art dealers and artists. Unset tables for simple meals, laid tables for elaborate Italian creations, and a long bar for exquisite cocktails.

Mon–Thurs 12.00–02.00, Fri/Sat to 03.00; Yorckstrasse 82, Kreuzberg; Tel. 786 29 89; Underground station: Mehringdamm; Bus: 119, 219

Café Savarin (F 5)

❋ A small, crowded *Kneipe* in an unprepossessing side street. The vegetable pies, quiches and salads are unbeatable.

Daily 10.00–24.00; Kulmer Strasse 17, Schöneberg; Tel. 216 38 64; Underground and S-Bahn station: Yorckstrasse

Einstein (T) (F 5)

❋ Old villa – even older than its film star owner, Henny Porten. Viennese coffee house and pretty garden downstairs; exhibitions upstairs. Attracts journalists and arty types. Cuisine and service in laid-back Austrian style.

Daily 10.00–02.00; Kurfürstenstrasse 58, Schöneberg; Tel. 261 50 96; Underground station: Kurfürstenstrasse, Nollendorfplatz

Hostaria del Monte Croce (G 5)

By the Kreuzberg, and Italian as the name suggests, eating in this unusual setting is a memorable experience. It is a country-style restaurant with long tables and benches, tucked away in the courtyard of a typical Berlin *Mietskaserne* (tenement block). The set menu is never-ending but moderately priced with generous portions. You will have plenty of time to get to know your neighbours.

Tues–Sat 19.30–24.00; second rear courtyard, Mittenwalder Strasse 6, Kreuzberg; Tel. 694 39 68; Underground station: Gneisenaustrasse

Kellerrestaurant im Brechthaus (G 3)

Next to the Dorotheenstädtischer Friedhof, where Bertholt Brecht is buried. Meals are prepared according to old Austrian recipes credited to Brecht's wife, Helene Weigel.

Gourmet restaurants

Bamberger Reiter (T)   (E 5)

An elegant setting where the dishes are sophisticated, always very tasty, but never cheap. The traditional German fare is served in ample portions. Set menu from 145 DM. You can eat for half the price in the bistro next door.
Tues–Sat from 18.00; Regensburger Strasse 7, Schöneberg; Tel. 218 42 82; Underground station: Spichernstrasse

First Floor, Palace Hotel   (E 4)

There are no limits to the culinary talents of Rolf Schmidt, one of Germany's top chefs. But his creations come at a price. Main course from 50 DM, set menu from 130 DM.
Mon–Sat (except Saturday lunchtime) 12.00–14.30 and 18.00–23.00; Budapester Strasse 42, Schöneberg; Tel. 25 02-0; Underground and S-Bahn station: Zoologischer Garten

Grand Slam   (O)

★ At the *Grün-Weiss* tennis club, Johannes King serves up some unforgettable food. Set menus from 135 DM.
Tues–Sat 18.00–22.00; Gottfried-von-Cramm-Weg 47–55, Dahlem; Tel. 825 38 10; Bus 119

Heising   (E 5)

This was where the *Ritz* once stood, and the restaurant has held on to its top-ranking spot. A friendly but intimate atmosphere, and the food is just perfect. Highly recommended, but advance booking essential. Set menu from 89 DM.
Mon–Sat from 19.00; Rankestrasse 32, Charlottenburg; Tel. 213 39 52; Underground station: Kurfürstendamm

Restaurant im Logenhaus (D 5)

A small restaurant tucked away in Wilmersdorf. Never advertises, as the chef, Jürgen Fehrenbach, needs no publicity. Classy, delicious and varied. Some German, some international influences. Always top quality. Set menu from 85 DM.
Mon–Sat 19.00–23.30; Emser Strasse 12–13, Wilmersdorf; Tel. 873 25 60; Underground station: Spichernstrasse

Rockendorfs Restaurant   (O)

Choose between a six-course set menu starting at 150 DM or one with nine courses from 200 DM, then add a little bit extra for the wine. Such Gargantuan feasts are hard to beat.
Tues–Sat (except public holidays) 12.00–14.00 and 19.00–21.30 (kitchen); Düsterhauptstrasse 1, Waidmannslust; Tel. 402 30 99; S-Bahn station: Waidmannslust

Vivaldi   (B 6)

Probably the most elegant and the most luxurious of Berlin's gastronomic temples. In the *Schlosshotel Vier Jahreszeiten*. Great garden for taking coffee. Main courses from 60 DM.
Hot meals from 18.30; Brahmsstrasse 6–10, Grunewald; Tel. 89 58 40; S-Bahn station: Grunewald; Bus: 129

Daily from 17.00; Chausseestrasse 125, Mitte; Tel. 282 38 42; Underground station: Oranienburger Tor

Metzer Eck   (H 3)
❧ An old Berlin *Kneipe* in Prenzlauer Berg, a fashionable meeting place for arty types from both East and West. Signed photos of art-world celebrities adorn the walls. Good pea soup and steaks help to ensure that the place is always crowded. Authentic old-fashioned feel.
Daily 16.00–01.00; Metzer Strasse 33, Prenzlauer Berg; Tel. 442 76 56; Underground station: Senefelderplatz

Offenbach-Stuben   (H–I 2)
Another down-to-earth artists' bar in Prenzlauer Berg, decorated with operatic memorabilia. Good food, extensive menu with traditional Berlin and German dishes and one or two more international offerings. Something of the old Democratic Republic lingers here – a bar for nostalgia lovers.
Daily from 18.00; Stubbenkammer Strasse 8, Prenzlauer Berg; Tel. 445 85 02; S-Bahn station: Prenzlauer Allee

Paris-Moskau (T)   (F 3)
🕏 By the railway line of the same name. A sort of level-crossing keeper's cottage – the last place you would expect to find an elegant restaurant for Berlin's gilded youth. Inside, everything is decked out smartly in black and white. Not the cheapest place to eat, but there are no grounds for complaint – the food is good and the portions ample.
Daily 18.00–24.00; Alt-Moabit 141, Tiergarten; Tel. 394 20 81; S-Bahn station: Lehrter Stadtbahnhof

Restauration 1900   (H 2)
★ At the renovated end of the Husemannstrasse. One of Prenzlauer Berg's 'in' bars. Always full, but sometimes it's just a bit too hectic. Small jokey menu and first-class spaghetti.
Daily 11.00–02.00; Husemannstrasse 1, Prenzlauer Berg; Tel. 442 24 94; Underground station: Senefelderplatz

Rosalinde   (D 4)
Upmarket *Kneipe* for students and young actors. Breakfast for late risers. Hot, mainly German fare served until late.
Daily 09.00-02.00; Knesebeckstrasse 16, Charlottenburg; Tel. 313 59 96; Underground station: Ernst-Reuter-Platz

Terzo Mondo   (D 4)
This restaurant may not look like much from the outside, but once inside, you'll feel very at home. Proprietor Kostas Papanastasiou, a star in *Lindenstrasse*, the famous

German TV soap opera, sometimes plays his guitar during the evenings.
Daily 18.00–03.30; Grolmannstrasse 28, Charlottenburg; Tel. 881 52 61; Underground station: Uhlandstrasse; S-Bahn station: Savignyplatz

Zur Letzten Instanz (H 4)

Founded in 1621 as a brandy bar, this is one of the city's oldest *Kneipen*. The stove and beer taps in its old-fashioned interior are over 200 years old. Among its more illustrious former guests were Napoleon, Mikhail Gorbachev, Charlie Chaplin, and Heinrich Zille. Try the *Eisbein* – Berlin-style knuckle of pork. Located near the municipal courts, all the dishes are given legal names, a reminder of the days when it was a popular haunt among judges and barristers.
Daily 12.00–01.00, Sun to 23.00; Waisenstrasse 14/16, Mitte; Tel. 242 55 28; Underground station: Klosterstrasse

CAFÉS & BREAKFAST BARS

Café am Neuen See (E 4)

❧ A Bavarian-style beer garden in the heart of the Tiergarten. Enjoy a hearty country breakfast, then hire a boat on the lake – you will scarcely believe that you are in the centre of Berlin.
Lichtensteinallee 1, Charlottenburg; Tel. 254 49 30; S-Bahn station: Tiergarten

Café im Literaturhaus (T) (D 5)

★ This villa, built by a sea captain in 1889, was extravagantly renovated, together with the neighbouring Kollwitz Museum and the Villa Griesebach, during the 1980s. It is now a tasteful, upmar-

ket coffee house and literary centre – a quiet and cultured oasis only a hundred yards from the Kurfürstendamm.
Daily 09.30–01.00; Fasanenstrasse 23, Charlottenburg; Tel. 882 54 14; Underground station: Kurfürstendamm

Café Schichulski (T) (E 6)

A quiet spot in the tranquil suburb of Friedenau. The place for those who need to start the day with a substantial breakfast.
Daily 09.30–01.00; Cosimaplatz 1, Friedenau; Tel. 851 66 84; Underground station: Friedrich-Wilhelm-Platz, Bundesplatz

Le Grand Café (G 4)

❧ In the *Grand Hotel* – an elegant café in an elegant location.
Daily 12.00–19.00; Friedrichstrasse 158–164 (Grand Hotel), Mitte; Tel. 20 27 32 03; Underground station: Friedrichstrasse

Möhring (T) (D 5 and G 4)

Quiet and rather formal, but just the place for relaxing over your

Indulge yourself in the Operncafé – from early in the morning until late at night

morning coffee. A wide variety of delicious gateaux is also available.
(**D5**) *Daily 07.00–24.00; Kurfürstendamm 213; Tel. 881 20 78; Underground station: Uhlandstrasse*
(**G4**) *Daily 08.00–24.00; Charlottenstrasse 50, am Gendarmenmarkt; Underground station: Französische Strasse*

Operncafé (G 4)
A palatial café in the traditional style located within the Opernpalais. Belongs to the *Wiener Kaffeehaus* chain. Their cakes are simply irresistible.
Daily 09.00–24.00; Unter den Linden 5, Mitte; Tel. 20 26 83; Underground station: Friedrichstrasse

Schwarzes Café (E 4)
⚲ Not to everyone's taste, but a popular hang-out among students and young people. Good music and food. Relaxed atmosphere. The 'Black Café' serves what's called a black special: black coffee, *Sobranie Black Russian* cigarette and black bread.
Daily 24 hrs (except Tues); Kantstrasse 148, Charlottenburg; Tel. 313 80 38; Underground station: Zoologischer Garten

RESTAURANTS

Category 1 (main course for one person 25–45 DM)

Abricot (H 6)
Fine food, classy service, sophisticated ambience and fine art on the walls. They certainly know how to cook in the Kreuzberg Kiez, and the prices are moderate, considering the high quality of the food.
Daily 12.00–01.00; Hasenheide 48, Kreuzberg; Tel. 693 11 50; Underground station: Südstern

Bacco (E 5)
One of Berlin's countless Italian eating houses, Bacco's has been a popular favourite for years. Mainly Tuscan fare.
Mon–Sat 12.00–15.00 and 18.00–24.00, Sun 18.00–24.00 (closed Sun in summer); Marburger Strasse 5, Charlottenburg; Tel. 211 86 87; Underground station: Wittenbergplatz

Don Camillo (T) (C 4)
Another well-established and highly-regarded Italian restaurant, with some excellent fish dishes on the menu, but prices are steep. A great garden terrace.
Mon–Sat 18.00–23.30; Schlossstrasse 7–8, Charlottenburg; Tel. 322 35 72; Underground station: Sophie-Charlotte-Platz

Fischküche (T) (D 5)
A new, chic and rather pricey fish restaurant, but still good value for money. In the peaceful Kempinski Plaza.
Mon–Fri 12.00–15.00 and 18.00–00.30, Sat 12.00–24.00; Uhlandstrasse 181–183, Charlottenburg; Tel. 882 48 62; Underground station: Uhlandstrasse

La Cascina (T) (C 6)
Bright rooms and large garden terrace in posh Grunewald, but unfortunately it stands on a busy road. The clientele and the food are equally upmarket. Always full on warm summer evenings. Book in advance.
Thurs–Tues 12.00–24.00; Delbrückstrasse 28, Grunewald; Tel. 826 17 94; Bus: 129, 110

Ponte Vecchio (C 4)
★ Italian restaurant with a reputation that extends well beyond Berlin's boundaries. It is not alto-

gether clear why, as the competition is stiff in this market. Prices are not extortionate and the customers remain loyal.

Wed–Mon 18.30–23.00; Spielhagenstrasse 3, Charlottenburg; Tel. 342 19 99; Underground station: Bismarckstrasse

Trio (C 4)

★ Small, simple and elegant. The ambitious proprietors offer nothing but the best, but at realistic prices. In the restored Charlottenburger Kiez.

Fri–Tues 19.00–01.00; Klausenerplatz 14, Charlottenburg; Tel. 321 77 82; S-Bahn station: Westend

Ugadawa (O)

This Japanese restaurant is less flashy than the very popular *Daitokai*, but not as expensive and much more authentic. At first glance it is just another Far Eastern restaurant, but on closer inspection it has an irresistible appeal. Off the beaten track in Steglitz.

Wed–Mon 17.30–23.30; Feuerbachstrasse 24, Steglitz; Tel. 792 23 73; Underground station: Walter-Schreiber-Platz

Zlata Praha (E 5)

Classy Czech restaurant that attracts a nouveau-riche clientele. The sizeable portions of hearty fare can be washed down with a cool Pilsener Urquell.

Daily 17.00–24.00; Meinekestrasse 4, Charlottenburg; Tel. 881 97 50; Underground station: Kurfürstendamm

Zur Goldenen Gans (G 4)

The 'Golden Goose' is one of the city's top restaurants, and is situated in *The Westin Grand Hotel*. Very swish, but with a rustic look. Serves traditional German fare,

with plenty of goose, red and green cabbage, potato dumplings, bacon salad and red wine. Berliners book in the autumn for Christmas.

Mon–Sat 18.00–24.00 (closed mid-July to beginning Sept); The Westin Grand Hotel, Friedrichstrasse 158–164, Mitte; Tel. 20 27 32 46; Underground station: Französische Strasse

Category 2 (main course for one person 20–35 DM)

Borchardt (T) (G 4)

★ A smart restaurant in a big high-ceilinged hall with mosaics and floor from the *Kaiserzeit*. Next to the Gendarmenmarkt in the Mitte district. Serves very acceptable food, and attracts celebrities in the evenings.

Daily 11.30–24.00; Französische Strasse 47, Mitte; Tel. 20 39 71 17; underground station: Französische Strasse

Fofi's Estiatorio (H 3)

This central spot attracts a cultured clientele who are happy to pay high prices for the pleasure of sitting in a delightful, informal ambience. The food may be no better than the Greek restaurant around the corner, but here it is the atmosphere that counts.

Daily 11.30–02.00; Rathausstrasse 25, Mitte; Tel. 242 34 35; Underground station: Alexanderplatz

Hakuin (E 5)

Japanese restaurant named after a Zen master, in a rather dull and run-down 1960s building, but the interior is something of a contrast. We recommend that you don't try to order fish from the artificial pond, as this is a strictly vegetarian restaurant! The dishes are very imaginative and tasty. A quiet, non-smoking establishment where advance booking is advisable.

Mon–Wed 16.00–23.30, Thurs–Sun 12.00–23.30; Martin-Luther-Strasse 1, Schöneberg; Tel. 218 20 27; Underground station: Wittenbergplatz

Hamlet (D 5)

A very pleasant bistro with imaginative French, as well as Arab-influenced cuisine. Great vegetable and salad dishes.

Daily 08.00–02.00; Uhlandstrasse 47, Wilmersdorf; Tel. 882 13 61; Underground station: Uhlandstrasse

Hardtke

✪ Since you probably didn't come to Berlin in search of Greek, Chinese, Italian or *nouvelle cuisine*, this is the place to come for traditional German fare. Try the *Eisbein, Jägerschnitzel, Filettopf,* or *Hackepeter* washed down with a good draught beer.

(**E4**) *Daily 11.00–24.00, Fri/Sat to 01.00; Meinekestrasse 27, Charlottenburg; Tel. 881 98 27; Underground station: Kurfürstendamm*

(**C6**) *Daily 12.00–24.00; Hubertusallee 48, Grunewald; Tel. 892 58 48; Bus: 129, 110*

Hitit (C 4)

The name refers to the ancient Hittite civilization of what is now southern Turkey, hence the reliefs and the waterfall. The food is upmarket Turkish, with a balanced menu of meat and vegetarian dishes, but is not too expensive. Situated in the attractive Charlottenburger Kiez.

Daily from 12.00, Sun–Thurs to 24.00, Fri/Sat to 01.00; Knobelsdorffstrasse 35, Charlottenburg; Tel. 322 45 57; Underground station: Sophie-Charlotte-Platz

Maxwell (T) (G 3)

★ Formerly in Wilmersdorf, this acclaimed restaurant has moved to a converted brewery in the Mitte district, but the prices are cheaper and the food even better.

Daily 12.00–24.00 (kitchen); Bergstrasse 22, Mitte; Tel. 280 71 21; Underground station: Rosenthaler Platz

Merhaba (T) (H 6)

★ 'Merhaba' is Turkish for 'hello' – and guests certainly receive a warm welcome in this bright and modern establishment. Prosperous Turkish families hold endless celebrations here. For more variety in your meal, you could opt for a selection of the starters instead of a main course.

Daily 15.00–01.00 (Sun from 12.00); Hasenheide 39, Kreuzberg; Tel. 692 17 13; Underground station: Südstern, Hermannsplatz

Paris Bar (E 4)

✪ Once a cheap student bar, now the clientele includes artists, writers and intellectuals. The food is French and quite expensive, but the place is still very popular.

Daily 12.00–02.00; Kantstrasse 152, Charlottenburg; Tel. 313 80 52; Underground station: Uhlandstrasse

Category 3 (main course for one person 15–30 DM)

Candela (E 6)

✦ ✪ At first glance, this does not look like an Italian restaurant, but there is no mistaking where the food originates from. A relaxed atmosphere is combined with excellent service.

Daily 17.00–01.00; Grunewaldstrasse 81, Schöneberg; Tel. 782 14 09; Underground station: Eisenacher Strasse

Carpe Diem (T)   (D 4)
One of many in a string of railway arches beneath the S-Bahn which have been converted into restaurants, bars and boutiques. Deliciously fresh *tapas* and imaginative main courses served with Spanish wine. Outside seating in the summer.
Tues–Sat 12.00–01.00 (except holidays); beneath the arches (no. 576) in the passageway between Uhlandstrasse and Grolmannstrasse; Tel. 313 27 28; S-Bahn station: Savignyplatz; Underground station: Uhlandstrasse

Grossbeerenkeller   (G 5)
❂ This culinary institution was founded in 1862, when Bismarck was prime minister under Kaiser Wilhelm I; the famous *Bismarckhering* (similar to rollmops) are still served here. This is the real Berlin.
Mon–Fri (except holidays) 16.00–02.00, Sat 18.00–02.00; Grossbeerenstrasse 90, Kreuzberg; Tel. 251 30 64; Underground station: Möckernbrücke

Mao Thai   (H 2)
Courteous service in friendly surroundings. Endless choice of Thai dishes, and all the items on the menu are of excellent quality.
Daily 12.00–14.00, 18.00–02.00; Wörther Strasse 30, Prenzlauer Berg; Tel. 441 92 61; Underground station: Senefelderplatz

Mutter Hoppe   (H 3)
A new-for-old bar and restaurant in the Nikolai-Viertel. Serves good, solid traditional Berlin fare and excellent draught beer. Centrally located.
Daily 11.30 onwards; Rathausstrasse 21, Mitte; Tel. 241 56 25; Underground station: Alexanderplatz

Oren   (G 3)
★ ❂ ☦ A very pleasant restaurant in the Jewish Cultural Centre next to the rebuilt Oranienburger Strasse synagogue. No meat dishes, but delicious fish. If you want to eat kosher though, go to the *Beth-Café* nearby.
Daily 10.00–01.00; Oranienburger Strasse 28, Mitte; Tel. 282 82 28; S-Bahn station: Oranienburger Strasse

Pasternak   (H 2)
This Russian restaurant is not a nostalgic throwback to the 'good old days'. It is relatively new and comfortable, and a great place to sample authentic Russian fare such as *borscht, pelmeni* and *blini*, washed down with quality wine.
Daily 12.00–02.00 (Sun from 10.00); Knaackstrasse 22–24, Prenzlauer Berg; Tel. 441 33 99; Underground station: Senefelder Platz

Tuk Tuk   (F 5)
☦ Simple and elaborate dishes are offered at reasonable prices, and served with consummate courtesy. It's a good idea to ascertain how hot and spicy your chosen dishes are before ordering.
Daily 17.00–01.00, kitchen closes 24.00; Grossgörschenstrasse 2, Schöneberg; Tel. 781 15 88; Underground station: Kleistpark

Zillemarkt (T)   (E 5)
☦ In an old garage at the heart of Berlin's restaurant district. Atmospheric *fin-de-siècle* garden, next to the Berlin–Moscow railway line. Call in for breakfast, lunch, newspapers, coffee and cakes – or late-night crêpes.
Daily 10.00–01.00, kitchen closes 24.00; Bleibtreustrasse 48a, Charlottenburg; Tel. 881 70 40; S-Bahn station: Savignyplatz

Shopping in style

Berlin has no shortage of haute couture and expensive jewellery, but it is also a great place for bric-à-brac, upmarket second-hand clothes and unusual gifts

When it comes to shopping, there is no denying that western Berlin is still literally streets ahead of the eastern side of the city. The main shopping areas are centred around Breidscheidtplatz and the ruined Gedächtniskirche (Memorial Church). Directly on Breidscheidtplatz stands the magnificent *Europa Center*, with about a hundred shops and restaurants, while Tauentzienstrasse, running east from the square, boasts the *Mini-City* with its trendy boutiques, together with numerous shoe shops and furniture stores and, at the eastern end near Wittenbergplatz, *KaDeWe* (*Kaufhaus des Westens* or 'Department Store for the West'), said to be the largest department store in continental Europe. To the west, the blackened ruin of the Gedächtniskirche also marks the start of the bustling Kurfürstendamm with its countless cafés, restaurants and fast-food outlets. Bookshops, hi-fi, photography and fashion shops also abound.

A gleaming new department store in Friedrichstrasse: Lafayette

Many people prefer to get away from the hectic atmosphere of the busy boulevards, and explore the side streets. Keithstrasse near Wittenbergplatz, for example, is renowned for its antique shops, while ★ Fasanenstrasse off the Kurfürstendamm is home to branches of *Cartier, Louis Vuitton, Champussy* and some upmarket antique shops. In the same area, Uhland-, Knesebeck- and, above all, ★ Bleibtreustrasse boast numerous outlandish boutiques and fashion jewellery and accessory stores, such as *Hotch Potch, Rose Rosa, Moosgrund, Soft, Kaufhaus Schrill* and *Lalique.* Keen browsers should head up towards the railway line at the northern end of Bleibtreustrasse and Knesebeckstrasse and explore the ★ ⚇ Savignypassage beneath the railway arches. For a lazy afternoon, take a stroll around the designer shops and bookstores, and then have a break in one of the *Kneipen,* such as *Bogen 597.*

Former East Berlin has seen the arrival of Western department stores and food chains. Friedrichstrasse will be the main luxury shopping street. The

59

Friedrichstadtpassagen and *Kaufhaus Lafayette* opened here in 1996, but they are only slowly coming to life. There are signs of a new dynamism in the Hackesche Höfe near Hackescher Markt underground station.

Most shops open around 09.00 or 10.00 and close on weekdays at 19.00 or 20.00, and on Saturdays at 16.00. Opening times are no longer strictly regulated, but shops have been slow to extend their trading hours. A few food shops in the city centre stay open until late, usually 22.00, eg on the Kurfürstendamm, at Fehrbelliner Platz, Schlossstrasse and Hermannstrasse underground stations, and at Tegel airport.

ANTIQUARIAN BOOKS

Düwal (D 6)
Regulars come here from far afield in search of first editions. Crammed full of books, with some real treasures among them.
Schlüterstrasse 17, Charlottenburg; S-Bahn station: Savignyplatz

Koch (E 4)
Many rare and precious items, plus great views of the city.
Kurfürstendamm 216, Charlottenburg; Underground station: Uhlandstrasse

Schomaker und Lehr (E 7)
Antiquarian art and literature: two shops, one address.
Niedstrasse 24, Friedenau; Underground station: Friedrich-Wilhelm-Platz

ANTIQUES

Berlin's antique shops are centred around Keithstrasse near Wittenbergplatz, around Fasanenstrasse and Bleibtreustrasse (both off the Kurfürstendamm), on Pariser Strasse, Pestalozzistrasse and Suarezstrasse (in Charlottenburg), as well as around Nollendorf- and Winterfeldplatz. A new antiques centre is emerging in the east of the city under the S-Bahn arches between Friedrichstrasse station and Kupfergraben. Here are just a few suggestions:

Art 1900 (D 5)
A centre for Jugendstil and Art Deco, selling furniture, pictures, ornaments, glassware and lamps.
Kurfürstendamm 53, Charlottenburg; Underground station: Adenauerplatz

A bookworm in Berlin is never short of places to explore

MARCO POLO SELECTION: SHOPPING

1 Bleibtreustrasse/Savigny-Passage
Wacky boutiques, great pubs (page 59)

2 Fasanenstrasse
Berlin's most exclusive shopping street (page 59)

3 KaDeWe
Top department store with unbelievable food hall (page 62)

4 Kaufhaus Schrill
For those with a penchant for bad taste and kitsch (page 65)

5 Pels Leusden
Renowned art gallery in an elegant 19th-century villa (page 62)

6 Rio
Stunning fashion jewellery and accessories (page 65)

7 Salumeria
Overflowing with Italian delicacies (page 65)

8 Schuhtick
Amazing shoe shop for those who like to stand out in a crowd (page 65)

9 Strasse des 17. Juni
Junk, bric-à-brac, art – and plenty of atmosphere (page 63)

10 Turkish market
A taste of the East beside the Landwehrkanal (page 64)

Lee (D 5)
Glassware, porcelain, ornaments – souvenirs at sensible prices.
Kurfürstendamm 32 (entrance in Uhlandstrasse), Charlottenburg; Underground station: Uhlandstrasse

Venzke (E 5)
Asian art: sculptures, jade, furniture and paintings from China and Japan.
Fasanenstrasse 71, Charlottenburg; Underground station: Uhlandstrasse

ART GALLERIES

Berlin has about 200 galleries: large and small, old-established and short-lived. Most of them are to be found in the west of the city, mainly on the Kurfürstendamm and its side streets. Sotheby's now has a branch by the Lustgarten. The *Berlin Programm* carries details of all current exhibitions.

Aedes (H 3)
Reputable architectural gallery in the Hackesche Höfe.
Rosenthaler Strasse 40–41, Mitte; S-Bahn station: Hackescher Markt

Art Galerie (D 5)
Christo, Dali, Hundertwasser, Wunderlich etc.
Kurfürstendamm 188, Charlottenburg; Underground station: Uhlandstrasse; bus 119

Bassenge (D 4)
Prints, views of the city, art and book auctions.
Bleibtreustrasse 19, Charlottenburg; S-Bahn station: Savignyplatz; Bus: 119

Brusberg (D 5)
Features predominantly (but not exclusively) ex-GDR artists.
Kurfürstendamm 213, Charlottenburg; Underground station: Uhlandstrasse

Galerie am Gendarmenmarkt (G 4)

Specializing in prints ranging from Toulouse-Lautrec to Zille.

Hilton Hotel, Mohrenstrasse 30, Mitte; Underground station: Stadtmitte

Nierendorf (E 4)

Modern classics.

Hardenbergstrasse 19, Charlottenburg; Underground station: Zoologischer Garten

Pels Leusden (D 5)

★ Specializes in art with an international interest. Located in the delightful 19th-century Villa Grisebach.

Fasanenstrasse 25, Charlottenburg; Underground station: Uhlandstrasse

COMICS

Grober Unfug (G 5)

⚥ Offers a fairly comprehensive range of German and international comics, with a sideline in gimmicky T-shirts. Often hosts exhibitions by well-known cartoonists in the gallery upstairs.

Zossener Strasse 32–33, Kreuzberg; Underground station: Gneisenaustrasse

DEPARTMENT STORES

Most districts in the east and west have their own branches of the chain stores *Hertie*, *Karstadt* and *Wertheim*, often within a stone's throw of each other. However, while lesser stores abound, there is only one ★ *KaDeWe*. With floor space totalling 60 000 sq m, this venerable Berlin institution is the largest store in Europe after *Harrods*. You can buy practically anything here, from antiques to the latest hi-tech gadgets. The store's real *tour de force* is undoubtedly the food department.

KaDeWe (E 5)

Tauentzienstrasse 21, Schöneberg; Underground station: Wittenbergplatz

Lafayette (G 4)

Corner of Friedrichstrasse and Französische Strasse, Mitte; Underground station: Französische Strasse

FASHION

Bramigk Design (D 4)

The place for fabrics. Nicola Bramigk, graduate of the Berlin Fashion School, specializes in Italian-designed materials. She also sells clothes designed in her own practical style, as well as colourful and comfortable slippers.

Savignypassage, Arch 598, Charlottenburg; S-Bahn station: Savignyplatz

Diva (D 4)

Great woollens – very smart and very unusual.

Goethestrasse 78, Charlottenburg; S-Bahn station: Savignyplatz

Kramberg (D 5)

Italian and US designs: Armani, Versace, Romeo Gigli, Donna Karan, plus Vivienne Westwood. Levi's a speciality. Not cheap, but very fashionable.

Kurfürstendamm 56–57, Charlottenburg; Underground station: Uhlandstrasse

Mientus (D 5)

Casual and formal menswear from Italy. Prices range from very reasonable to extortionate.

Kurfürstendamm 52, Charlottenburg; Underground station: Uhlandstrasse

Molotow (G 5)

Nowhere supplies Berlin designs at better prices. Over 20 local designers show off their collections

The Eco-Markt in Dahlem

here. Clothes can also be made to customer's specifications.
Gneisenaustrasse 112, Kreuzberg; Underground station: Mehringdamm

Ralf Setzer (D 5)

Tasteful, classic, top-quality menswear. The women's fashions on sale in the sister store follow the same formula.
Kurfürstendamm 46 and Bleibtreustrasse 19, both Charlottenburg; Underground station: Uhlandstrasse

Berlin's biggest and best flea market is to be found on ★ Strasse des 17. Juni (*Sat/Sun 10.00–17.00; Underground station: Ernst-Reuter-Platz; S-Bahn station: Tiergarten*). You will find some good art and crafts on sale amid the piles of junk and bric-a-brac. Other weekend flea markets are held between the Zeughaus and Kupfergraben (*Sat/Sun 11.00–17.00; underground and S-Bahn station: Friedrichstrasse*), and by the water tower in Kopischstrasse (*Sun 10.00–15.00; Under-*

ground station: Platz der Luftbrücke). For slightly better quality, 'Old-Berlin' bric-a-brac, try the Zille-Hof in Fasanenstrasse. Antiques, artwork, jumble, and odds and ends are sold in the S-Bahn arches along Georgenstrasse.
Wed–Mon 11.00–18.00; Arches 190–203; Underground and S-Bahn station: Friedrichstrasse

Fanshop (E 4)

A marvellous variety of souvenirs and gifts.
Budapester Strasse 46, Charlottenburg; Underground station: Zoologischer Garten

Gipsformerei
Staatliche Museen (C 3)

Stocks over 6000 casts of sculptures from every period in history. You can even take a copy of the legendary *Bust of Queen Nefertiti* home with you.
Sophie-Charlotten-Strasse 17–18, Charlottenburg; S-Bahn station: Westend

Königliche Porzellan-Manufaktur (E 4)

This wonderful old china shop, founded in 1763, is the place to come for that special dinner service, vase or set of figurines.

Wegelystrasse 1, Tiergarten; S-Bahn station: Tiergarten

MARKETS

All districts in Berlin have their own produce markets. The best ones are: Rathaus Schöneberg (*Tues and Fri 08.00–13.00*), Wittenbergplatz (*Tues and Fri 08.00–14.00*), and outside the Rotes Rathaus in the Mitte district (*Tues 09.00–17.00, Sat 08.00–14.00*). The traditional indoor markets convey some of the atmosphere of 'Old Berlin' and the most interesting ones are at Marheinekeplatz in Bergmannstrasse (*Mon–Fri 08.00– 18.00, Sat 08.00–13.00*), in the Arminiusmarkthalle (*Mon–Fri 07.30–18.00, Sat 07.30–13.00*) near Turmstrasse, and the Eco-Market on Königin-Luise-Strasse in Dahlem (*Sat 08.00–13.00*).

Winterfeldmarkt (F 5)

☆ A typical Berlin market by a church with plenty of shops and cafés round about. The stalls overflow with a wide range of goods sold by noisy market traders and inspected by a critical, streetwise clientele. It's the epitome of the Schöneberg scene: casual, informal and self-confident.

Winterfeldplatz, Schöneberg; Wed and Sat 08.00–14.00; Underground station: Nollendorfplatz

Maybachufer market (H–I 5)

★ The produce sold at this colourful Turkish market is guaranteed to be good quality. Turkish shoppers are very discerning and know how to appreciate fresh fruit and vegetables, tasty spices, crumbly ewe's milk cheese, and oven-warm bread. Here, on the boundary between the two main Turkish quarters of Kreuzberg and Neukölln, it is easy to imagine that you are in Istanbul.

Maybachufer, Kreuzberg; Tues and Fri 12.00–18.30; Underground station: Kottbusser Tor

MUSIC, CDS & TAPES

Canzone (D 4)

Records, tapes and CDs from all over the world.

Savignypassage, Arch 583, Charlottenburg; S-Bahn station: Savignyplatz

Fidelio (F 6)

A treasure trove for collectors of classical and jazz music.

Akazienstrasse 30, Schöneberg; Underground station: Eisenacher Strasse

Wegert (E 5)

An extremely large store full of CDs, videos and hi-fi equipment. Well-catalogued, but still somewhat bewildering.

Kurfürstendamm 202–206 (in the Ku'damm-Karree), Charlottenburg; Underground station: Uhlandstrasse

ODDS & ENDS/ACCESSORIES

Bergmannstrasse (G 5–6)

The *Ararat Curiosity Shop* and the Marheinekeplatz market hall, both situated in Kreuzberg's Bergmannstrasse, are guaranteed to keep you amused for an hour or two. Trendy junk stalls, jewellery, fashion, and unusual bits and pieces.

Bergmannstrasse, Kreuzberg; Underground station: Gneisenaustrasse

Kaufhaus Schrill (D 5)
★ If you want a pig embroidered on your tie, or crocodiles on your briefs, this is the place to come to.
Bleibtreustrasse 46, Charlottenburg; S-Bahn station: Savignyplatz

Knopf-Paul (G 4)
More than a million buttons of every size and description to rummage through. You may find it hard to resist buying a whole assortment, even though you have no specific use for them!
Zossener Strasse 10, Kreuzberg; Underground station: Gneisenaustrasse

Rio (D 4)
★ Fashion jewellery made from colourful beads, glass and diamanté, wire, stones, imitation gold and silver. Some items are made on the premises, some hail from much further afield.
Bleibtreustrasse 52, Charlottenburg; S-Bahn station: Savignyplatz

SHOES

Bruno Magli (D 5)
The finest in classic Italian shoes. Expensive but very stylish, particularly the ladies' shoes.
Kurfürstendamm 62, Charlottenburg; Underground station: Adenauerplatz

Schuhtick
★ This shoe store chain has several branches, all of which offer an incredible range of footwear, from the classic and fashionable to the wild and wacky.
(D4) *Savignyplatz 11, Charlottenburg; S-Bahn station: Savignyplatz*
(E5) *Tauentzienstrasse 5, Schöneberg; Underground station: Wittenbergplatz*
(H3) *Karl-Liebknecht-Strasse, Mitte; underground and S-Bahn station: Alexanderplatz*

SPECIALITY FOODS

The food hall in *KaDeWe* department store in Tauentzienstrasse has an amazing range of delicacies and specialities imported from all over the world – lobsters, caviar, cheese, preserves, exotic fruit, vegetables, and more than 1000 varieties of German sausage. If *KaDeWe* still hasn't got what you are looking for, the following stores all have their own specialities:

King's Teagarden (D 5)
Tea and all the trappings: a wide range of teapots, tea caddies etc.
Kurfürstendamm 217, Charlottenburg; Underground station: Uhlandstrasse

Marzipankonditorei Wald (C 4)
Following recipes originating from their East Prussian homeland, Irmgard and Paul Wald produce delicious sweets and desserts in the kitchen behind their tiny shop.
Pestalozzistrasse 54a, Charlottenburg; Underground station: Sophie-Charlotte-Platz

Rogacki (D 4)
Fish smoke house. Offers both catering and party service, plus a restaurant where you can enjoy the flavourful fish.
Wilmersdorfer Strasse 145, Charlottenburg; Underground station: Bismarckstrasse

Salumeria (C 4)
★ The best Italian fare including hams, cheese, antipasti, wines, and always a few new delicacies to sample.
Windscheidstrasse 20; Underground station: Wilmersdorfer Strasse

A good night's sleep

Few beds are ever empty despite all the tourist hotels built after reunification

Ever since the Wall came down people have been flocking to Berlin in their hundreds of thousands: politicians, business executives, traders, speculators, tourists and backpackers. Berlin has always been worth a visit, but now everyone wants to come here, some to play a part in the action, but most just to see the dynamic new city for themselves; to witness the unique historical process that is taking place. The city is fast developing into a sophisticated cultural metropolis – into a capital city that forms a bridge between East and West.

The consequence of so much rapid change is that Berlin is more overcrowded than it has ever been. Not just during the trade fairs, exhibitions and conferences, but all the time. While many new hotels have been built to accommodate the huge influx, you should still reserve your accommodation well in advance. The city has certainly not been slow in

The Hotel Radisson SAS, situated opposite the Berliner Dom and the Rotes Rathaus

responding to the increased demand. The luxurious *Hilton* and *Four Seasons* have opened on the Gendarmenmarkt, while the grand, sophisticated *Estrel Residence & Congress Hotel* has opened its doors in Neukölln; the top-ranking *Hotel Adlon* on Pariser Platz is newly completed. And there is so much planning and building still going on – possibly more than will ultimately be justified by the demand.

The hotel industry is experiencing much the same difficulties as other sectors. Change is taking place so rapidly in the former East Berlin that new, privately-run guest houses and hotels are springing up all over the place, only to disappear as quickly as they came. Given that there are at least 450 establishments, the list of recommended hotels in this chapter is by no means exhaustive, though it should certainly prove useful. The most coveted of Berlin's 50 000 or so hotel beds get booked up well in advance. However, when choosing a hotel, do bear in mind that establishments classified as mid-range often have very high standards, while some of the cheaper hotels offer extremely good value for money. For most hotels and guest houses, the prices given include breakfast. Stated tariffs apply for a single room; for a double room add an extra 30%.

For further information about the city's hotels, and a hotel booking service, contact one of the tourist information offices:

Europa Center (**E4**)*, Budapester Strasse; Mon–Sat 08.00–22.00, Sun 09.00–21.00; Brandenburger Tor* (**G4**)*, daily 09.30–18.00; Tegel Airport* (**C1**)*, main hall (near the Lufthansa desk), daily 05.15–22.00.*

Postal address: Berlin Tourismus Marketing GmbH, Am Karlsbad 11, 10785 Berlin, Telephone hotline: 25 00 25, Fax 25 00 24 24.

Tourist offices should also have information on youth hostels. Alternatively, you can contact the Berlin headquarters of the German Youth Hostel Association:

Deutsches Jugendherbergswerk (**G5**)*, Tempelhofer Ufer 2, Kreuzberg; Tel. 262 30 24; Mon–Thurs 08.00–15.00, Fri 08.00–14.00*

CATEGORY A HOTELS

(DM 230–450)

Cecilienhof (O)
★ Palace hotel on a historic site near Potsdam. Exudes a certain old-fashioned charm. 42 rooms.
Neuer Garten, 14469 Potsdam; Tel. 0331/370 50, Fax 0331/29 24 98; S-Bahn station: Potsdam Stadt

Excelsior (E 4)
Excellent hotel, good restaurants, near Bahnhof Zoo. 318 rooms.
Hardenbergstrasse 14, 10623 Berlin; Tel. 31 55-0, Fax 31 55 10 02; Underground station: Zoologischer Garten

Four Seasons Hotel (G 4)
★ A luxurious new hotel in a historic location. Good restaurant and friendly staff. 204 rooms.
Charlottenstrasse 49, 10117 Berlin; Tel. 203 38; Underground station: Französische Strasse

Holiday Inn Crowne Plaza (E 5)
Pleasant hotel near Tauentzienstrasse. Room price does not include breakfast. 425 rooms.
Nürnberger Strasse 65, 10787 Berlin; Tel. 21 00 70, Fax 213 20 09; Underground station: Wittenbergplatz

Mondial (D 5)
★ A very pleasant, well-kept hotel, fully equipped for the disabled with bathing and care facilities. The Kräutergarten restaurant is highly acclaimed. 85 rooms.
Kurfürstendamm 47, 10707 Berlin, Tel. 88 41 10, Fax 88 41 11 50; Underground station: Uhlandstrasse

Radisson SAS (H 3)
Between the Berliner Dom and the Marienkirche in the heart of historic Berlin. Every imaginable comfort. 540 rooms.
Karl-Liebknecht-Strasse 5, 10178 Berlin; Tel. 23 82-8, Fax 23 82 75 90; Underground station: Alexanderplatz

Savoy Hotel (E 4)
★ Not large, but rather stylish. Between the Ku'damm and the zoo. Only a short walk from the Berliner Börse (stock exchange). Price does not include breakfast. 125 rooms.
Fasanenstrasse 9–10, 10623 Berlin; Tel. 311 03-0, Fax 31 10 33 33; Underground station: Zoologischer Garten

Seehof (C 4)
★ Pleasant hotel, not too large, and not far from the ICC (Inter-

MARCO POLO SELECTION: HOTELS

1 Cecilienhof
Spend the night in a royal chamber (page 68)

2 Dittberner
Good value for money at this guest house (page 70)

3 Forsthaus Hubertusbrücke
In a tranquil spot near the Düppel Forest and the Stölpchensee (page 69)

4 Four Seasons Hotel
Relax in comfort near the historic Gendarmenmarkt (page 68)

5 Igel
A small, family-run concern out in the country (page 71)

6 Kronprinz
Comfortable rooms in a 19th-century setting (page 69)

7 Mondial
A well-equipped hotel which caters for the disabled (page 68)

8 Paulsborn
You can be sure of an undisturbed night in the Grunewald (page 70)

9 Savoy Hotel
Pleasant and stylish hotel close to city centre (page 68)

10 Seehof
Intimate atmosphere by the Lietzensee (page 68)

national Congress Centre). Views of the Lietzensee. 77 rooms.
Lietzenseeufer 11, 14057 Berlin; Tel. 32 00 20, Fax 32 00 22 51; Bus: 149; S-Bahn station: Witzleben

Steigenberger (E 5)
Large hotel with a very discerning clientele. Very comfortable suites. The *Park-Restaurant* is highly regarded. 397 rooms.
Los-Angeles-Platz 1, 10789 Berlin; Tel. 212 70, Fax 212 71 17; Underground station: Kurfürstendamm

CATEGORY B HOTELS

(DM 150–250)

Forsthaus Hubertusbrücke (0)
★ In a quiet spot about half way between Potsdam and the city centre. 22 rooms.
Stölpchenweg 45, 14109 Berlin; Tel. 805 30 00, Fax 805 35 24; Bus: 118; S-Bahn station: Wannsee

Imperial (D 5)
In the heart of the entertainment district. A good mid-range hotel with a garden terrace and swimming pool. 81 rooms.
Lietzenburger Strasse 79–81, 10719 Berlin; Tel. 880 05-0, Fax 382 45 79; Underground station: Uhlandstrasse

Kardell (D 4)
Quality hotel with a restaurant renowned for its Berlin specialities. 33 rooms.
Gervinusstrasse 24, 10629 Berlin; Tel. 324 10 66, Fax 324 97 10; Underground station: Adenauerplatz

Kronprinz (D 5)
★ Comfortable rooms in a fully renovated *Gründerzeit* residence. At the western end of the Kurfürstendamm near the Messegelände. 72 rooms.
Kronprinzendamm 1, 10711 Berlin; Tel. 89 60 30, Fax 893 12 15; Underground station: Adenauerplatz

The tradition of grand hotels lives on in the Schlosshotel Vier Jahreszeiten

Paulsborn (O)

★ Very quiet setting in a forest lodge in the Grunewald known as the *Forsthaus Paulsborn*. Cosy rustic interior and a recommended restaurant, popular with weekend walkers. Large garden terrace. 10 rooms.

Am Grunewaldsee, entrance from Hüttenweg, 14193 Berlin; Tel. 813 80 10, Fax 814 11 56

Rheinsberg am See (O)

Way up in the north of the city, by a small lake in the Wittenau district. A very pleasant hotel with indoor and outdoor swimming pools. 81 rooms.

Finsterwalder Strasse 64, 13435 Berlin; Tel. 402 10 02, Fax 403 50 57; S-Bahn station: Wittenau Nord

Wittelsbach (D 5)

Quiet and child friendly. Central location. Breakfast room for non-smokers. Good value for money. 34 rooms.

Wittelsbacherstrasse 22, 10707 Berlin; Tel. 861 43 71 or 873 63 45, Fax 862 15 32; Underground station: Konstanzer Strasse

CATEGORY C HOTELS

(DM 90–180)

Artemisia (D 5)

The only women's hotel in Berlin – no men allowed. 8 rooms.

Brandenburgische Strasse 18, 10707 Berlin; Tel. 873 89 05, 873 63 73, Fax 861 86 53; Underground station: Konstanzer Strasse

Belvedere (B 6)

In a villa near the Kurfürstendamm. Affordable, but price does not include breakfast. 17 rooms.

Seebergsteig 4, 14193 Berlin; Tel. 82 60 01-0, Fax 82 60 01 63; Bus: 129, 119

Bogota (D 5)

Quiet, inexpensive, yet close to the Kurfürstendamm. 130 rooms.

Schlüterstrasse 45, 10707 Berlin; Tel. 881 50 01, Fax 883 58 87; Underground station: Uhlandstrasse

Dittberner (D 5)

★ Just off the Kurfürstendamm. Above-average comfort at a sensible price. 22 rooms.

Wielandstrasse 26, 10707 Berlin; Tel. 881 64 85, 88 46 95-0, Fax 885 40 46; Underground station: Adenauerplatz

Heidelberg (D 4)
Bed and breakfast hotel, close to the Ku'damm. 40 rooms.
Knesebeckstrasse 15, 10623 Berlin; Tel. 313 01 03, Fax 313 58 70; Underground station: Ernst-Reuter-Platz

Igel (O)
★ A smallish, modern hotel under family management. In a quiet location, near Tegel lake and forest. 67 rooms.
Frederikestrasse 33–34, 13505 Berlin; Tel. 436 00 10, 431 40 42, Fax 436 24 70; Bus: 222

Majestic (D 5)
Well-maintained, quiet hotel with own parking. Close to the Ku'damm. Bed and breakfast. 48 rooms.
Brandenburgische Strasse 47, 10707 Berlin; Tel. 891 90 76, Fax 891 90 73; Underground station: Fehrbelliner Platz

---

Berlin's luxury hotels

Bristol Hotel Kempinski (D 5)
Traditionally, Berlin's premier hotel. By the busy Kurfürstendamm, but rooms are quiet. Superior decor and hushed atmosphere. This is where celebrities from the worlds of politics, art and showbiz stay. Prices do not include breakfast. 315 rooms, from 340 DM.
Kurfürstendamm 27, 10719 Berlin; Tel. 884 34-0, Fax 883 60 75; Underground station: Kurfürstendamm

Hotel Adlon (G 4)
Near the Brandenburg Gate. The epitome of luxury in an exclusive district. 337 rooms, from 420 DM.
Unter den Linden 77, 10117 Berlin; Tel. 101 17, Fax 22 61 22 22; Underground station: Unter den Linden

Grand Hotel Esplanade (F 4)
A luxury, post-modern hotel beside the Landwehrkanal. All the latest amenities; even has its own landing stage. Not in the smartest of locations, though. 402 rooms, from 380 DM.
Lützowufer 15, 10785 Berlin; Tel. 26 10 11, Fax 265 11 71; Bus X9

Inter-Continental (E 4)
In the Budapester Strasse hotel quarter. Luxury American-style accommodation which attracts a lot of foreign guests. Prices do not include breakfast. 511 rooms, from 295 DM.
Budapester Strasse 2, 10787 Berlin; Tel. 260 20, Fax 260 28 07 60; Underground station: Zoologischer Garten

Schlosshotel Vier Jahreszeiten (B 6)
Extravagantly restored under the direction of Karl Lagerfeld. Listed building in the exclusive Grunewald district near the Ku'-damm. 52 rooms, from 545 DM.
Brahmsstrasse 10, 14193 Berlin; Tel. 89 58 40, Fax 89 58 48 00; Bus 119, 129

Modena (D 5)
Inexpensive, well-run guest house in a quiet spot near the Ku'damm. 21 rooms.
Wielandstrasse 26, 10707 Berlin; Tel. 881 52 94, 885 70 10, Fax 881 52 94; Underground station: Adenauerplatz

Savigny (D 5)
Simple and inexpensive, but clean and tidy. 52 rooms.
Brandenburgische Strasse 21, 10707 Berlin; Tel. 881 30 01, Fax 882 55 19; Underground station: Konstanzer Strasse

Sylvia (O)
Small apartment hotel not far from Dahlem. All rooms have a bath. Heated swimming pool. Price does not include breakfast. 18 rooms.
Warnemünder Strasse 19, 14199 Berlin; Tel. 823 30 71, Fax 824 40 35; Bus: 110

SHORT-TERM LETS

Mitwohnzentralen are agencies that will find rooms for people wishing to stay in Berlin for anything from a week to six months. During the summer, for example, flats and rooms become available when the permanent resident, perhaps a student, goes away on holiday or to work. Some of these agencies specialize in rooms for women travelling alone. A modest commission is payable, based on the cost of the room or flat. Rents usually work out cheaper than the cost of a hotel.

Addresses:
Last Minute, Tel. 30 82 08 85/6, Fax 30 82 08 87; Mitwohnzentrale Holsteinische Strasse 55, Tel. 861 82 22, Fax 861 82 72; Mitwohnzentrale Yorckstrasse 52, Tel. 194 30, Fax 216 94 01

BUDGET ACCOMMODATION

Young people can find cheap accommodation in the state-run hostels, which are often in attractive woodland settings. For more information, contact the local district office (*Bezirksämter*). Most of the western district councils run hostels in the green suburbs. There are 17 other hostels, which provide cheap accommodation for youth groups and young independent travellers. Contact the tourist information office for details. For youth hostels, contact the German

The Bristol Hotel Kempinski is one of Berlin's finest

Come as you are

In general, Berliners like to dress casually. While formal dress is expected in banks and boardrooms, you will see comparatively few people on the street dressed in sombre suits and ties; even secretaries of state have been known to turn up for work in trainers. If you decide to splash out on a smart restaurant, then of course smart clothes are appropriate. Otherwise, casual is fine.

If you are invited into a Berliner's home for an evening meal, you won't be expected to dress up but you will be expected to be punctual. It is customary to take something with you as a gift: flowers for the lady of the house, perhaps, and a bottle of wine, especially for informal gatherings.

Youth Hostel Headquarters.
Berlin Tourist-Information, Europa Center, 10789 Berlin; Tel. 25 00 25; or am Karlsbad 11; Tel. 26 47 48-12, Fax 26 47 48-99
Deutsches Jugendherbergswerk, Tempelhofer Ufer 32, Kreuzberg, 10963 Berlin; Tel. 264 95 20. Central reservations: Kluckstrasse 3, 10785 Berlin; Tel. 262 30 24, Fax 262 95 29

Jugendgästehaus am Wannsee (0)
A few tent pitches also available.
Badeweg 1, 14129 Berlin; Tel. 803 20 34, Fax 803 59 08; S-Bahn station: Nikolassee

Jugendgästehaus Berlin (F 5)
Kluckstrasse 3, 10785 Berlin; Tel. 261 10 97/98, Fax 265 03 83; Underground station: Kurfürstenstrasse, Bülowstrasse

Jugendherberge Ernst-Reuter (0)
Hermsdorfer Damm 48, 13467 Berlin; Tel. 404 16 10, Fax 404 59 72; S-Bahn station: Hermsdorf

CAMPSITES

Berlin has a number of well-equipped campsites in attractive locations, but nearly all of them are on the edge of the city and difficult to reach by public transport. Worth considering if you have your own transport.

Camping Kladow (0)
Beside Lake Havel. Best facilities of all the Berlin sites.
Krampnitzer Weg 111–17, Spandau; Tel. 365 27 97; Underground station: Rathaus Spandau, then bus 134 and 234

Camping Dreilinden (0)
In the south-west of the city.
Albrechts Teerofen, Zehlendorf; Tel. 805 12 01; Underground station: Oskar-Helene-Heim, then Bus 118 and walk or take a taxi

Camping Krossinsee (0)
Only campsite in the east of the city. Pleasant spot near the lakes.
Wernsdorfer Strasse 45, Köpenick; Tel. 675 86 87; S-Bahn station: Grünar, then tram 68 and bus E-25

Zeltlagerplatz (0)
For student groups only.
Inselstrasse 7, Schwanenwerder, Wannsee; S-Bahn station: Nikolassee Summer booking onsite, Tel. 803 62 47; in winter via Bezirksamt Steglitz, Youth and Sport Dept., Tel. 79 04 46 80/81/82, Fax 79 04 45 45

The Berlin calendar

*With a cultural calendar that's packed with events,
exhibitions, festivals and sporting fixtures,
it's impossible to get bored in Berlin*

Whatever the time of year, there is always something going on somewhere in this lively city. The really big events – such as the ★ Berlin Philharmonic playing at the Waldbühne, the huge 'Love Parade' street party, or world-famous rock bands playing the Olympia-Stadion – draw massive crowds from far and wide.

The city's grand old palaces provide elegant venues for classical music concerts. Performances are frequently staged in the Remisenhof at Schloss Glienicke, in the sumptuous surroundings of Schloss Charlottenburg, and at Schloss Friedrichsfelde. A particularly popular annual event is the Brandenburgische Sommerkonzerte – a series of summer concerts held in the churches and palaces of the Mark Brandenburg.

The less high-profile events, however, can be just as much fun. In summer you may well stumble upon a street festival in some corner of the city, where you can join the locals for a few beers, a bite to eat and some music. Various community festivals are held all year round, ranging from the Britzer Baumblütenfest (Blossom Festival), the Turmstrassenfest, the Kreuzberger Festliche Tage, and the Tierparkfest to the Köpenicker Sommer, the Weissenseer Blumenfest (Flower Festival) and on to the many *Weihnachtsmärkte* (Christmas fairs) held throughout the city in the run-up to Christmas. At Whitsuntide, even habitual late risers get up early, so as not to miss out on the morning concerts held in the zoos, parks and country cafés. Just before midnight on New Year's Eve, crowds of warmly wrapped people head for the 'mountains': the Teufelsberg (120 m), the Insulaner (75 m), and the ★ ☙ Kreuzberg (66 m) to watch giant fireworks displays.

PUBLIC HOLIDAYS

1 January *New Year's Day*
Good Friday
Easter Monday
1 May *May Day*
Ascension Day

The Berlin music scene is alive with young musicians playing in pubs, former cinemas and in the open air

MARCO POLO SELECTION: EVENTS

1 Berliner Festwochen
A whole month of interna-
tional cultural events – one
of Berlin's biggest attractions
(page 77)

**2 Brandenburgische
Sommerkonzerte**
Music performed in churches
and palaces, lectures, picnics
(page 77)

3 JazzFest Berlin
Four nights of music with the
best jazz bands in the world
(page 77)

**4 New Year's Eve on the
Kreuzberg**
Chilled bubbly, hot pancakes,
dazzling fireworks, and warm
embraces (page 75)

**5 Philharmonic concerts at the
Waldbühne open-air stage**
Classical music *al fresco*,
conducted by top conductor
Claudio Abbado (page 75)

6 Theatertreffen
A whole series of top German
. theatrical productions
(page 76)

Whit Monday
3 October *Reunification Day*
3rd Wednesday in November *Day
of Prayer and National Repentance*
24 December *Christmas Eve*
25 December *Christmas Day*
26 December *Boxing Day*

SPECIAL EVENTS

January
❂ *Grüne Woche*. Held at the
Messegelände, this is Berlin's
annual agricultural show. See the
prize pigs and cattle, and sample
the oysters, sausages, cheeses and
other gourmet delights from
around the world.

February
Internationale Filmfestspiele. Berlin's
international film festival is the
biggest in the world after Cannes
and Venice. Twelve days of back-
to-back movies, old and new,
mainstream and art house, most
of which are shown with their
original soundtracks, ie not
dubbed into German.

March
Internationale Tourismusbörse. Tourism fair at the Messegelände featuring holiday information and
freebies from around the globe.

April
Import Shop. A trade fair for developing countries to show off their
arts and crafts.

May
★ *Theatertreffen*. A number of different theatre companies stage
productions and hold discussions.
Mainly German-speaking.
ⵝ *Theatertreffen der Jugend*. Youth
drama festival.

June
Deutsches Pokalendspiel. German
Football Cup Final.
Christopher Street Day. A parade to
mark Gay Action Week.

June/July
*Open Air Classic Hoppegarten;
Glienicker Schlosskonzerte*. Two
treats for lovers of classical music.

July

Jazz in July. At the Quasimodo.
Classic Open Air. Concerts on the Gendarmenmarkt.
☥ *Love Parade.* Ravers from all over Europe transform the city into one huge techno party zone.

July / August

Heimatklänge. Third World musicians perform in the Haus der Kulturen and the Tempodrom.
★ *Brandenburgische Sommerkonzerte.* From the end of June until the end of August, classical and religious music in the finest churches and palaces in and around Berlin.

August / September

❖ *Internationale Funkausstellung.* A broadcast media extravaganza held every other year.
★ *Berliner Festwochen.* An arts festival on a grand scale.

September

❖ ☥ *Oktoberfest.* Something of a misnomer, as it begins in the middle of September.
Berlin Marathon. On the first Sunday of the month, tens of thousands of runners descend on the city for this race, which starts on Strasse des 17. Juni, takes a tour of the suburbs, and finishes at the Gedächtniskirche.

October

☥ *Jazz-Treff.* Three days in which the Berlin jazz scene displays its multitude of talents. The main venue is the Musikinstrumenten-museum. *Bus: 149*

November

★ *JazzFest Berlin.* Five days and nights of top-class jazz.
☥ Young musicians and young writers festival.
☥ *Children's Theatre Week,* with over 100 performances.
Jüdische Kulturtage. Festival of Jewish culture.

December

❖ *Weihnachtsmärkte.* Christmas markets in many parts of the city, including Europa Center and Spandau Altstadt.

INFORMATION

Berlin festivals: Tel. 25 48 90, Fax 25 48 91 11
Brandenburgische Sommerkonzerte: Tel. 89 69 06-30, Fax -40
Classic Open Air: Tel. 247 35 90
Glienicker Schlosskonzerte: Tel. 821 60 09

International Congress Centre and Radio Tower

Out on the town

From culture vultures to techno fans –
Berlin has something for everyone

The Philharmonie, the Schau-spielhaus, five stages for opera and musicals, more than 80 main-stream, alternative, and children's theatres, 20 cabarets, over 100 cinemas, any number of jazz, rock and folk clubs – Berlin's cul-tural menu caters for all tastes, from the simplest to the most dis-cerning. The city has its sights set on becoming an international cultural metropolis, but it is still too early to tell to what extent it can realistically achieve this aim. Competition is fierce between the many arts companies in the city. State subsidies are dwindling fast, and private sponsorships are increasingly difficult to come by. That said, Berlin's cultural scene is thriving. Just as in the 1920s, the cultures of eastern, central, and western Europe are combin-ing to produce great entertain-ment for all.

As well as following the listed recommendations, it's worth ex-ploring the side streets to make some discoveries of your own.

Berlin provides a stage for numerous experimental theatre groups

BALLET – MUSICALS – OPERA

Deutsche Oper Berlin   (D 4)
★ Highly acclaimed perform-ances by top international stars.
Bismarckstrasse 35, Charlottenburg; Tel. 341 02 49; Underground station: Deutsche Oper

Komische Oper   (G 4)
Under the lasting influence of Walter Felsenstein, the 'Comic Opera House' has become less traditional, and is much cheaper than its main competitor. The mixed operatic repertoire also in-cludes classical ballet.
Behrenstrasse 55–57, Mitte; Tel. 47 02 10 00 and 0180/530 41 68; Un-derground station: Friedrichstrasse

Neuköllner Oper   (O)
✦ Young artists stage their own witty productions, most of which are surprisingly professional.
Karl-Marx-Strasse 131–133, Neu-kölln; Tel. 68 89 07 77; Underground station: Karl-Marx-Strasse

Staatsoper Unter den Linden (G 4)
★ Classical repertoire in Kno-belsdorff's grand theatre. The opera house dates from 1742. It will take some time before the

79

The Friedrichstadtpalast – Europe's newest revue theatre

productions can once again match the grandeur of the building, but progress is being made.

Unter den Linden 7, Mitte; Tel. 20 35 45 55; Underground and S-Bahn station: Friedrichstrasse; Bus: 100, 157, 349

Theater des Westens (E 4)

Musicals and operetta. Has produced some long-running box-office hits such as *La Cage aux Folles* and *Hello Dolly*, performed by home-grown talent.

Kantstrasse 12, Charlottenburg; Tel. 882 28 88; Underground station: Zoologischer Garten

BARS

Champussy (D 5)

Sophisticated spot in Berlin's most elegant shopping quarter.

Daily from 19.00; Uhlandstrasse 171/172, Wilmersdorf; Tel. 881 22 20; Underground station: Uhlandstrasse

Galerie Bremer (D 5)

Art gallery by day, artists' rendezvous by night. White-haired Rudi from the Dutch Antilles has worked here for decades and is now a fully-fledged Berliner.

Fasanenstrasse 37, Wilmersdorf; Tel. 881 49 08; Underground station: Uhlandstrasse

Harry's New York Bar (F 4)

In the *Hotel Esplanade*. Tries hard to emulate the real thing.

Lützowufer 15, Schöneberg; Tel. 25 47 88 21; Bus: 100, 129, 187, 341

DANCE CLUBS

Abraxas (D 4)

Hot and steamy Latin American beats: salsa and samba at deafening volume. This venue is rather small and crowded, but lots of fun and very popular.

Kantstrasse 134, Charlottenburg; Tel. 312 94 93; S-Bahn station: Savignyplatz

Akba Lounge (H 2)

Out the back of the bar and up the stairs, this is a sophisticated club with lots of atmosphere. Acid jazz, soul and pop.

Sredzkistrasse 64, Prenzlauer Berg; Tel. 441 14 63; S-Bahn station: Prenzlauer Berg

Clärchens Ballhaus (G 3)

✪ A traditional style dance club, the walls of which are decorated

ENTERTAINMENT

MARCO POLO SELECTION: ENTERTAINMENT

1 Berliner Ensemble
Following in the footsteps of
Bertholt Brecht (page 87)

2 Deutsche Oper Berlin
Spectacular performances on
a tight budget (page 79)

3 Staatsoper Unter den Linden
Once the Royal Court
Opera, still a grand building
(page 79)

4 Filmkunst 66
Cult cinema showing cult
films (page 83)

5 90 Grad
Wild and exuberant,
lots of fun (page 81)

6 Friedrichstadtpalast
All-singing, all-dancing,
shows (page 86)

7 Grips-Theater
Far more than just a youth
theatre (page 87)

8 Philharmonie
Even without the masterful
Karajan, the Philharmonie
still has a magical appeal
(page 84)

9 Quasimodo
For many years, the city's top
venue for jazz (page 86)

10 Schaubühne
Still Berlin's top theatre
(page 88)

with drawings by Zille. A dance band turns out the old favourites. An entertaining spot for singles – you may well be asked to dance.
Auguststrasse 24, Mitte; Tel. 282 92 95; Underground station: Rosenthaler Platz

Knaack-Club Berlin   **(I 2)**
🕺 This is what Kreuzberg used to be like: punters dressed in black, with punk haircuts, drinking bottled beer and listening to rock and dance music. The disco in the cellar downstairs is almost always full to bursting. Live bands.
Greifswalder Strasse 224, Prenzlauer Berg; Tel. 442 70 60; Bus: 100, Tram: 2,3,4

Metropol   **(F 5)**
🕺 The place to be – if you have just turned 17. Berlin's biggest disco, complete with lasers and all

the Euro-disco trimmings, is housed in a lovely Art Deco building. Hip hop and house etc. with the occasional live band.
Nollendorfplatz 5, Schöneberg; Tel. 21 73 68 41; Underground station: Nollendorfplatz

Roter Salon/Volksbühne   **(H 3)**
Tango Wednesday nights, fifties music Friday nights, offbeat and wacky every night.
Rosa-Luxemburg-Platz, Mitte; Tel. 30 87 48 06; Underground station: Rosa-Luxemburg-Platz

90 Grad   **(F 5)**
★ Berlin meets New York. House and funk, drag queen beauty pageant on Thursdays. Full of thirty-somethings.
Dennewitzstrasse 37, Tiergarten; Tel. 262 89 84; Underground station: Bülowstrasse

CABARET

Once upon a time, Berlin was Germany's cabaret centre, but the Nazis disapproved of the artists' extravagant political satire and sexual licence. Since the war, club owners have been trying to revive the tradition. East Berlin's *Die Distel* ('The Thistle') was popular with audiences, but not with the GDR government. Now the GDR has gone, but *Die Distel* is still there. West Berlin's *Stachelschweine* ('Porcupines') has an equally long pedigree, but it has lost some of its sting these days – there simply isn't very much left to poke fun at. The newer, alternative cabarets in Kreuzberg are much more acerbic and risqué. Admission charges can be high.

BKA and BKA im Zelt

The *Berliner Kabarett Anstalt* attracts artists from all over Germany. Interesting shows.
(**G5**) *Mehringdamm 32–34, Kreuzberg; Tel. 251 01 12; Underground station: Mehringdamm; Marquee* (**F4**) *An der Philharmonie, Tiergarten; Bus: N5, N29, N52, 129, 148, 348*

Die Distel (G 3)

Up until 1989, East Berlin's best-known cabaret could only get away with very mild political satire. Now it's no holds barred.
Friedrichstrasse 101, Mitte; Tel. 204 47 04; Underground and S-Bahn station: Friedrichstrasse

Kartoon (G 4)

Do the waiters work as cabaret artists, or are the cabaret artists part-time waiters?
Französische Strasse 24, Mitte; Tel. 204 47 56; Underground station: Französische Strasse

Stachelschweine (E 4)

Once known for its biting humour, the 'porcupine's satire' is now rather blunted. Probably the only place in Berlin where Honecker and his cronies are missed.
Europa Center, Tauentzienstrasse, Charlottenburg; Tel. 261 47 95; Underground station: Zoologischer Garten

Ufa-Fabrik (0)

ホ 'Culture factory' which offers a whole range of different entertainments and activities: children's circus, variety, jazz, Tai Chi sessions, etc. Worth investigating.
Viktoriastrasse 13, Tempelhof; Tel. 75 50 30; Underground station: Ullsteinstrasse

CHILDREN'S THEATRE

Most of the shows put on in the following venues are very visual, and can still be enjoyed by children who don't speak German.

Berliner Figurentheater (F 5)

Puppet theatre.
ホ *Yorckstrasse 59, Kreuzberg; Tel. 786 98 15; Underground station: Yorckstrasse*

Hans Wurst Nachfahren (F 5)

ホ *Gleditschstrasse 5, entrance from Winterfeldplatz, Schöneberg; Tel. 216 79 25; Underground station: Nollendorfplatz; Bus: 119*

Klecks-Kindertheater (H 5)

Puppet theatre.
ホ *Schinkestrasse 8–9, Neukölln; Tel. 693 77 31; Underground station: Schönleinstrasse*

Puppentheater-Museum (I 6)

ホ *Karl-Marx-Strasse 135, Neukölln; Tel. 687 81 32; Underground: Karl-Marx-Strasse*

Zaubertheater Igor Jedlin (D 5)
Roscherstrasse 7, Charlottenburg; Tel. 323 37 77; Underground station: Adenauerplatz

CINEMAS

Berlin's lively film scene keeps going throughout the year, although it receives a boost in February from the International Film Festival. Two days a week, usually Tuesday and Wednesday, tickets are sold at cheap rates. Film fans with no knowledge of German need not despair: if a film is listed as *OF* or *OV*, then it is shown in its original language; *OmU* means in its original language but with German subtitles. Occasionally, films are screened *OmE* – original with English subtitles.

Cinema Paris (D 5)
The city's top mainstream cinema screens premières of the major commercial releases.
Kurfürstendamm 211, Charlottenburg; Tel. 881 31 19; Underground station: Uhlandstrasse

Filmbühne am Steinplatz (D 4)
Arts cinema with a varied and interesting programme. Nice café.
Hardenbergstrasse 12, Charlottenburg; Tel. 312 90 12; Underground station: Zoologischer Garten

Filmkunst 66 and 66 1/2 (D4–5)
★ As well as showing all the latest releases, this cinema often screens rare cult films.
Bleibtreustrasse 12, Charlottenburg; Tel. 882 17 53; S-Bahn station: Savignyplatz

Graffiti (E 5)
A popular venue for rare and unusual films.

Pariser Strasse 44, Charlottenburg; Tel. 88 68 33 22; Underground station: Spichernstrasse

International (H 3)
Large cinema in the heart of East Berlin – another venue for premières.
Karl-Marx-Allee 33, corner of Schillingstrasse; Tel. 242 58 26; Underground station: Schillingstrasse

Kant (D 4)
☆ Two-screen cinema showing the latest releases.
Kantstrasse 54, Charlottenburg; Tel. 312 50 47; Underground station: Wilmersdorfer Strasse

Kurbel (D 5)
Three screens; all films shown in their original language.
Giesebrechtstrasse 4, Charlottenburg; Tel. 883 53 25; Underground station: Adenauerplatz

Lupe 1 and Lupe 2 (D 5)
Two pleasant, moderately-sized film theatres. Good programme.
Kurfürstendamm 202, Charlottenburg; Tel. 883 61 06; Underground station: Uhlandstrasse; Olivaer Platz 15, Charlottenburg; Tel. 882 37 77; Underground station: Adenauerplatz

Marmorhaus (E 5)
Sometimes shows premières, but generally rather downmarket.
Kurfürstendamm 236, Charlottenburg; Tel. 881 15 22; Underground station: Kurfürstendamm

New Yorck/Yorck (G 5)
☆ Fashionable cinemas in Riehmers Hofgarten. No advance booking.
Yorckstrasse 86, Kreuzberg; Tel. 78 91 32 40; Underground station: Mehringdamm

Zeughaus (G 4)

Rare pre- and post-war films in a historic setting.

Unter den Linden 2, Mitte; Tel. 215 02-0; Underground and S-Bahn station: Friedrichstrasse

CONCERTS

With Claudio Abbado as artistic director, the Berlin Philharmonic, based in the Philharmonie on Kemperplatz, goes from strength to strength; meanwhile in the Schauspielhaus on the Gendarmenmarkt, the Berlin Symphony Orchestra has matured into one of the world's leading ensembles under conductor Vladimir Ashkenazy. However, the Berlin music scene extends well beyond these two great orchestras: there are plenty of smaller companies, chamber orchestras, choirs and soloists. All the world's great orchestras relish playing here. To find out what's on, consult the *Berlin Programm* (free from tourist offices) or buy one of the listings magazines: *Zitty*, *Tip* or *Prinz*.

Philharmonie and Kammermusiksaal (F 4)

★ *Matthäikirchstrasse 1, Schöneberg; Tel. 254 88-0; Bus: 129, 142, 148, 248*

Konzerthaus Berlin (G 4)

Gendarmenmarkt, Mitte; Tel. 203 09 21 01/02; Underground station: Stadtmitte, Hausvogteiplatz

JAZZ & ROCK

Berlin has exponents of practically every musical direction: there are thousands of amateur musicians, a few hundred semi-professionals, but unfortunately only a handful of really talented professionals. Top international musicians on tour usually include Berlin in their itineraries, as they can attract sizeable audiences. Events range from gigs in pub cellars to the prestigious 'Jazz in July' and 'JazzFest Berlin' festivals, and big-name bands at the Waldbühne and the ICC congress centre. Berlin audiences are enthusiastic and well-informed.

Jewish Berlin

In 1933, Berlin had a Jewish population of about 170 000, some 5% of the total. The lucky ones managed to leave Germany in the 1930s, but during the war approximately 50 000 Jewish Berliners were deported and murdered by the Nazis, while others were hidden away by non-Jewish citizens. The present Jewish population is slightly more than 10 000, a number which is gradually increasing as Jews from eastern European countries emigrate in search of a higher standard of living.

In November 1989, when the Berlin Wall fell, the Jewish community in the GDR numbered a mere 200; yet it is there, in the area around Oranienburger Strasse, that most of the Jewish institutions are located: the New Synagogue, the Centrum Judaicum, the schools, the *Oren* restaurant, *Beth Café*, and so on. Other reminders of Berlin's once-flourishing Jewish community are provided by the city's Jewish cemeteries and synagogues.

One of the world's finest concert halls: Scharoun's Philharmonie

A Trane (D 4)

Small, but good jazz club, featuring home-grown and international talent.

Pestalozzistrasse 105, Charlottenburg; Tel. 313 25 50; S-Bahn station: Savignyplatz

Aue (E 6)

✪ Art gallery and *Kneipe*. Mainstream jazz every Sunday from lunchtime onwards.

Berliner Strasse 48, Wilmersdorf; Tel. 873 49 76; Underground station: Blissestrasse

Badenscher Hof (E 6)

Modern jazz, and mainstream, in an intimate atmosphere.

Badensche Strasse 29, Schöneberg; Tel. 861 00 80; Underground station: Berliner Strasse

Eierschale 1 and Eierschale Zenner (O)

✪ Pop and rock during the week, dixieland at the weekend. Always full. Friendly audience. Free disco before and after the bands.

Podbielskiallee 50, Dahlem; Tel. 832 70 97; Underground station: Podbielskiallee; Alt-Treptow 14–17, Treptow; Tel. 533 73 70; S-Bahn station: Treptower Park

Ewige Lampe (D 4)

Typical Berlin corner-*Kneipe*. Trad jazz on Saturdays.

Niebuhrstrasse 11a, Charlottenburg; Tel. 324 39 18; S-Bahn station: Savignyplatz

Kleine Weltlaterne (D 5)

New Orleans jazz on Saturdays and various other times.

Nestorstrasse 22, Wilmersdorf; Tel. 892 65 85; Underground station: Adenauerplatz

MS Sanssouci (I 5)

On a ship permanently moored at the Oberbaumbrücke. The Berlin jazz scene meets here for jam sessions on Wednesdays. Disco on Fridays and Saturdays.

Gröbenufer, Kreuzberg; Tel. 611 12 55; Underground station: Schlesisches Tor

Podewil (H 4)

Jazz, world music, even classical concerts. Less lively than some other venues, but they take their music seriously here.

Klosterstrasse 68–70, Mitte; Tel. 24 74 96; Underground station: Klosterstrasse

Quasimodo (E 4)

★ Continues to be Berlin's top jazz club. Small and usually packed to the rafters. Top international stars, predominantly American, perform here, as well as lesser-known, but very accomplished musicians.

Kantstrasse 12a, Charlottenburg; Tel. 312 80 86; Underground station: Zoologischer Garten

Yorckschlösschen (G 5)

An unusual *Kneipe* with old-time jazz on Sundays.

Yorckstrasse 15, Kreuzberg; Tel. 215 80 70; Underground station: Mehringdamm

REVUES & VARIETY

In this sector of the entertainments industry, the GDR's Friedrichstrasse was on a par with the best in the world – and much of it has survived.

Bar jeder Vernunft (E 5)

Reckoned by many to be Berlin's best. By the old Volksbühne.

Schaperstrasse 24, Wilmersdorf; Tel. 883 15 82; Underground station: Spichernstrasse

Chamäleon (H 3)

The restored Hackesche Höfe building with its Jugendstil façade and old dance hall is the ideal venue for variety shows. Berliners love the clowns, acrobats and magicians.

Rosenthaler Strasse 40/41, Mitte; Tel. 282 71 18; S-Bahn station: Hackescher Markt; Underground station: Weinmeisterstrasse

Friedrichstadtpalast (G 3)

★ Berlin's most famous nightspot. The main revue is a class act made up of variety performances, an extravagant floor show, and loud music. The atmosphere in the smaller revue theatre tends to be more intimate.

Friedrichstrasse 107, Mitte; Tel. 232 62-0, 232 62-474; Underground and S-Bahn station: Friedrichstrasse

La Vie en Rose (O)

Revue theatre with glamorous girls, terrific tightrope-walkers, and marvellous magicians.

Platz der Luftbrücke, Tempelhof (left of airport entrance); Tel. 69 51 30 00; Underground station: Platz der Luftbrücke

Tempodrom (F 3)

❖ A Berlin institution. Attractions include circus acts, rock, jazz, and world music, dance, and open-air food stalls. Will be displaced when work starts on the new government buildings.

Tent park, Tiergarten; Tel. 394 40 45; S-Bahn station: Lehrter Bahnhof

Tränenpalast (G 3)

The old departure terminal at Friedrichstrasse station (where GDR citizens with valid exit permits left for the West). Now a fashionable venue for cabaret, jazz, salsa, celebrity parties, and fashion shows.

Corner Friedrichstrasse/Reichstagsufer, Mitte; Tel. 238 62 11; Underground station: Friedrichstrasse

Wintergarten (F 5)

International stars from the world of variety play to packed houses. Late-night entertainment at high prices.

Potsdamer Strasse 96, Tiergarten (ticket sales via Berlin-Ticket); Tel. 23 08 82 30; Underground station: Kurfürstenstrasse

THEATRE – MAINSTREAM

Now that the Wall has gone, the two halves of the Berlin theatre scene are slowly growing back together again. Many areas overlap or are duplicated – opera, musicals, political satire, puppet theatres etc. However, that poses few problems, as the catchment area for audiences has grown, and Berlin continues to draw in more and more business people, politicians and, of course, tourists. The theatres of the East have had to make radical changes to their repertoires, in order to appeal to a new public. Another problem that all of Berlin's theatre companies face is that the city council's dwindling subsidies do not go very far, when there are so many takers. The Schiller-Theater, for one, has had to make major cutbacks in recent years, and will not be the last theatre to feel the pinch. Few of the plays are in English, though some groups do occasionally put on performances for foreign tourists.

Berliner Ensemble (G 3)

★ Where Brecht's *Threepenny Opera* was first performed. For many years during the GDR era, this theatre was mainly used for staging other works by the great master. Now it is a venue for modern drama, although the frequent changes in management have affected the quality of the productions.

Bertholt-Brecht-Platz, Mitte; Tel. 282 31 60; Underground station: Friedrichstrasse

Deutsches Theater (G 3–4)

The varied repertoire includes German classics and works by modern playwrights. One of Berlin's best theatres, and almost always sold out.

Schumannstrasse 10/13a, Mitte; Tel. 28 44 12 25/6; Underground station: Friedrichstrasse

Grips-Theater (E 3–4)

★ Volker Ludwig has transformed this children's and young people's theatre into a Berlin institution.

Altonaer Strasse 22, Tiergarten; Tel. 391 40 04; Underground station: Hansaplatz

Komödie/Theater am Kurfürstendamm (D 5)

Light comedy, much of it of British origin.

Kurfürstendamm 206, Charlottenburg; Tel. 47 02 10 10; Underground station: Uhlandstrasse

Maxim Gorki Theater (G 3)

Don't be misled by the theatre's name: as well as works by Russian playwrights, American and German dramatists feature prominently as well.

Am Festungsgraben 2, Mitte; Tel. 20 22 11 15, 20 22 11 29; Underground station: Friedrichstrasse; S-Bahn station: Hackescher Markt

Renaissance Theater (D 4)

Private theatre with a sound reputation.

Hardenbergstrasse 6, Charlottenburg; Tel. 312 42 02; Underground station: Ernst-Reuter-Platz

Schaubühne (D 5)

★ Still a first-class theatre that nearly always plays to full houses.

Kurfürstendamm 153, Wilmersdorf; Tel. 89 00 23; Underground station: Adenauerplatz

Schiller-Theater (D 4)

Wide-ranging repertoire. No longer has its own ensemble: mainly a venue for travelling companies and musicals.

Bismarckstrasse 110, Charlottenburg; Tel. 31 11 31 11; Underground station: Ernst-Reuter-Platz

Volksbühne (H 3)

Cutting edge political theatre.

Rosa-Luxemburg-Platz, Mitte; Tel. 247 67 72/308 74-661; Underground station: Rosa-Luxemburg-Platz

THEATRE – ALTERNATIVE

In Berlin as elsewhere, experimental and alternative theatre companies inhabit a transient world. Nothing ever stays in one place for long, but that makes Berlin's *Szene* all the more exhilarating. Consult the free *Berlin Programm* or the magazines *Tip* and *Zitty* for up-to-date listings.

The Schaubühne theatre

Kleines Theater (D 7)

A lightweight programme. Over the top, erotic – and very popular.

Südwestkorso 64, Schöneberg; Tel. 821 30 30; Underground station: Rüdesheimer Platz

Ratibor Theater (I 5)

Well-established fringe theatre.

Cuvrystrasse 20, Kreuzberg; Tel. 618 61 99; Underground station: Schlesisches Tor

Teatr Kreatur (G 5)

Colourful, imaginative, and always stimulating.

Tempelhofer Ufer 10; Tel. 251 31 16; Underground station: Möckernbrücke

Theater zum westlichen Stadthirschen (G 5)

A veritable hotbed of dramatic energy and enthusiasm.

Kreuzbergstrasse 37, Kreuzberg; Tel. 785 70 33; Underground station: Yorckstrasse

Zan Pollo Theater (0)

A versatile company with a great sense of humour.

Rheinstrasse 45, Steglitz; Tel. 852 20 02; Underground station: Walter-Schreiber-Platz

Practical information

Useful addresses and information for your trip to Berlin

BANKS & CHANGING MONEY

Banks are open from Monday to Friday, and some on the Kurfürstendamm open on Saturday too. Banking hours vary widely, but most banks open on weekdays at 09.00, and on Saturday at 10.00, closing between about 12.00 and 15.00, except for Tuesdays and Thursdays when many of them stay open until 18.00.

*Bureau de change at Bahnhof Zoo (**E4**) Mon–Sat 07.30–22.00, Sun and public holidays 08.00–21.00. ATM*

CAR PARKING

Parking in the city centre is becoming more and more difficult. Vehicles parked carelessly will be towed away, and retrieval can cost as much as 200 DM. In some areas, a rationing system operates, with rates varying between 2 and 4 DM per hour. The larger hotels have adequate car parking, and in the centre of West Berlin there are multi-storey car parks. The largest are in Uhlandstrasse, Kantstrasse, Fasanenstrasse, and behind the Europa Center. Fees are usually 3 DM per hour, or upwards of 15 DM for a whole day.

EMBASSIES/CONSULATES

Britain
Unter den Linden 32–34, Mitte; Tel. (00 49 30) 20 18 40

Eire
Ernst-Reuter-Platz 10, Charlottenburg; Tel. (00 49 30) 348 00 80

US
Neustädtischer Kirchstrasse 4–5, Mitte; Tel. (011 49 30) 238 51 74

EMERGENCY & HELPLINE NUMBERS

Emergency services
Ambulance: 192 000
Police: 110
Fire brigade: 112

Medical emergencies
Emergency dentist: Tel. 89 00 43 33
24-hr emergency doctor: Tel. 31 00 31

Crisis lines
Samaritans: Tel. 0800/1110111
Women's crisis centre: 615 42 43, 615 75 96

Emergency breakdown services
ACE: 01802/34 35 36
ADAC: 01802/22 22 22

HAIRDRESSERS

Most luxury hotels have salons which are open to non-residents. Berlin's top hairdresser is located in the Kempinski Plaza:

Udo Walz (D 5)
Kurfürstendamm 200, Charlotten-burg; Tel. 881 15 40; Underground station: Uhlandstrasse

LOST & FOUND

Police (G 6)
Platz der Luftbrücke 6, Tempelhof; Tel. 699-5; Underground station: Platz der Luftbrücke

Railways/S-Bahn (H 3)
Hackescher Markt, Mitte; Tel. 29 72 96 12

BVG (Berlin underground and bus service operator) (O)
Lorenzweg 5, Tempelhof; Tel. 25 62 30 40

MEDICAL MATTERS

Citizens of EU member countries are entitled to free medical care in Germany. To be eligible, however, UK citizens are required to produce an E111 form, otherwise treatment will be charged for. You can obtain one of these forms from a main post office, although an additional private health, accident, and theft insurance policy is always recommended.

PASSPORTS/VISAS

For EU citizens a valid passport or national identity is enough to secure entry into the country. Holders of Australian, Canadian, Japanese, New Zealand, South African and US passports are automatically permitted to stay for three months before they need to apply for a Visa.

POST/TELEPHONES

Berlin's main post offices are open Mon–Fri 08.00–18.00, Sat 08.00–12.00 or 13.00. Extended opening hours apply at Tegel airport *(daily 07.00–21.00)*, at Strasse der Pariser Commune *(daily 08.00–22.00)*, and at Friedrichshain *(daily 07.00-21.00)*. At Bahnhof Zoo post office, counters are open Mon–Sat 06.00–24.00, Sun and public holidays 08.00–24.00. The poste restante service for Berlin is based here. *Tel. 311 00 20*

To make an international call, dial 00 followed by the country code (*UK: 44, US: 1, Eire: 353*), then the area code omitting the initial 0, followed by the subscriber number. You can make international calls from most phone boxes in the city, but nearly all of them accept phone cards only. These are available from post offices and some shops.

PUBLIC TRANSPORT

The Berlin public transport network is fast, clean and safe, although it is better to avoid empty carriages when travelling at night. The two Berlin transport companies have amalgamated to form the BVG and the two systems are now thoroughly integrated. The suburban railway network (S-Bahn) is now operated by the German National Railway Company (Bundesbahn). The BVG runs the underground (U-Bahn), the bus services and the eastern-Berlin tram service.

Within the BVG area, underground trains and bus services start at 04.00 or 04.30 and continue until 00.15 and 01.00. The S-Bahn runs until about 23.30, in some cases until 01.00. On Friday and Saturday, the underground service on lines 9 and 12 runs throughout the night.

There are three tariff zones: A is the inner city area within the S-Bahn circle line, B is all of Berlin as far as the city boundary, C the surrounding area as far as Potsdam. Single tickets for two tariff zones cost 3.60 DM, for three zones 3.90 DM, for children 2.40 or 2.60 DM respectively. A 24-hour ticket costs 7.50/8.50 DM. The Welcome-Card is another attractive option for visitors: it entitles one adult and up to three children to travel on the BVG network for 72 hours, and costs 29 DM (price includes discount on admission to many museums, theatres, and other attractions). For details, contact tourist information offices or BVG ticket offices. For information about group tickets, contact the BVG customer service department, *Tel. 194 49.*

Berlin Public Transport Authority (Berliner-Verkehrs-Betriebe) (F 5)
Potsdamer Strasse 188, Schöneberg; Tel. 256-0; Underground station: Kleistpark

Information helplines
Airports: Schönefeld (Russia and eastern Europe): 60 91-0; Tegel (rest of Europe and long-haul): 41 01-1; information: 41 01-23 06; Tempelhof (domestic and charter flights): 69 51-22 88
Bus station: 301 80 28, 302 52 94
Train times (Bundesbahn): 194 19

Telebus operates a special service for disabled people requiring transport to and from sporting and cultural events. *Tel. 41 02 00, Fax 41 02 02 50*

SIGHTSEEING

If you want to take a sightseeing tour in Berlin, there are four main companies which all provide remarkably similar tours at remarkably similar prices. Full tours cost from 39 to 47 DM, shorter tours are 30 DM, and trips to Potsdam are 54 DM. Many of the tours only run during the summer.
Operators:
Bus-Verkehr Berlin: departure from Kurfürstendamm 225; Tel. 885 98 80, Fax 881 35 08
Severin + Kühn: departure from Kurfürstendamm 216; Tel. 880 41 90, Fax 882 56 18
Berliner Bären Stadtrundfahrt: departure from Rankestrasse/corner of Kurfürstendamm and from Alexanderplatz; Tel. 35 19 52-70, Fax -90
Berolina Sightseeing, departure from Kurfürstendamm 220; Tel. 882 20 91/92, 88 56 80 30, Fax 882 41 28

Perhaps of more interest are the historical city tours, which explore various themes such as 'Berlin 1800', 'Literary Berlin', 'City of Fashion', etc.
Stattreisen, Tel. 455 30 28
Schölzel, Tel. 395 97 99
Stadtkontor, Tel. 262 91 14

If you are prepared to pay more for individual attention, Kaibel & Erdmann arrange tailor-made tours. *Tel. 661 01 27*

As well as cruises on the Havel or the Potsdam lakes, trips along Berlin's rivers and canals make interesting excursions.

Boat companies:
Stern- und Kreisschiffahrt: Tel. 53 63 60-0/803 10 55, Fax 53 63 60 99
Riedel: Tel. 691 37 82, Fax 694 21 91
Triebler: Tel. 331 54 14
Spreefahrt: Tel. 394 49 54
Winkler: Tel. 391 63 08

TAXIS

There is no shortage of taxis in Berlin. Only when the weather is poor, or if some major event is taking place, might it prove difficult to find one. Taxis can be hailed anywhere in the city. The basic charge is 4 DM for the first kilometre and then up to 2.30 DM for each subsequent kilometre (up to 2.40 DM per km between 23.00 and 06.00). A journey from Tegel Airport to the city centre will cost about 30 DM.
Funk Taxi: 26 10 26
Spree Funk: 44 33 22
Taxi Funk: 690 22
Würfelfunk: 21 01 01

THEATRE TICKETS

Most good hotels will obtain theatre tickets for their guests, but if you want to hear the Berlin Philharmonic it is always better to book a seat in advance, preferably before you leave home.

East Berlin stages are currently complaining about a drop in audience figures, so most of the theatres there will have tickets to sell on the night. Ticket agencies add a surcharge of between 10 and 15% to the ticket price. The Kant-Kasse specializes in jazz concerts.
KaDeWe Showtime: Tel. 217 77 54, Fax 825 21 61
Kant-Kasse: Tel. 313 45 54, Fax 312 64 40
Last Minute: Tel. 242 67 09

Hekticket: Tel. 883 60 10, 243 12 431
Telefonischer Kartenversand: Tel. 615 88 18, 615 89 18, Fax 615 87 19

TIME

Germany is 6 hours ahead of US Eastern Standard Time and 1 hour ahead of Greenwich Mean Time.

TIPPING

Restaurant and café prices are inclusive of service, but if the food and service are of an acceptable standard, many people leave an added tip of between 5 and 10%. The norm for taxi drivers is around 10%. Hairdressers and hotel staff expect a tip of 2–3 DM, sometimes more, depending on the quality of the hotel. Toilet attendants leave a saucer out for small contributions.

TOURIST INFORMATION

Tourist Information Offices
UK:
65 Curzon Street, London WIY 7PE; Tel. 0171-493 0080 or 0891-600100 (recorded message)
US:
747 Third Avenue, 33rd Floor, New York, NY 10017; Tel. 212-308 3300
Berlin:
Europa Center, Budapester Strasse; Mon–Sat 08.00–22.00, Sun 09.00–21.00
Brandenburger Tor, Pariser Platz; daily 09.30–18.00
Tegel Airport, computerized Infopoint
Bahnhof Zoo; daily 08.00–22.30
Telephone hotline: 25 00 25, Fax 25 00 24 24
Postal address: *Berlin Tourismus Marketing GmbH, Am Karlsbad 11, 10785 Berlin*

WHAT'S ON

The listings magazines *Tip* (*http://www.tip-berlin.de*) and *Zitty* are both published fortnightly, in German only. They provide a comprehensive overview of Berlin's sporting and cultural calendar. As well as a full listings service for eastern Berlin, western Berlin and Potsdam, they give information on ticket prices, transport details, and a brief critical evaluation (for those whose German is up to it). The section giving venue addresses and telephone numbers is always up to date. The monthly German-language *Berlin Programm* is not quite so detailed, but is available free from tourist offices. *Führer durch die Konzertsäle Berlins* specializes in the music scene. *Berlin das Magazin* is published quarterly in German and English. *Berlin tut gut* is published in English, and is available from tourist information offices.

Berlin Tourismus Marketing GmbH, Am Karlsbad 11, 10785 Berlin, also provides details about concerts, theatres, exhibitions and sporting events. For more information about events, entertainment and eating out, take a look at the Berlin Online website: *http://www.BerlinOnline.de*.

WEATHER IN BERLIN

Seasonal averages

Daytime temperatures in °C

Jan	Feb	Mar	Apr	May	June	July	Aug	Sep	Oct	Nov	Dec
2	3	8	13	19	22	24	23	19	13	7	3

Night-time temperatures in °C

Jan	Feb	Mar	Apr	May	June	July	Aug	Sep	Oct	Nov	Dec
-3	-3	0	4	8	12	14	13	10	6	2	-1

Sunshine: hours per day

Jan	Feb	Mar	Apr	May	June	July	Aug	Sep	Oct	Nov	Dec
2	3	5	6	8	8	8	7	6	4	2	1

Rainfall: days per month

Jan	Feb	Mar	Apr	May	June	July	Aug	Sep	Oct	Nov	Dec
11	9	8	9	9	9	11	9	8	9	10	9

Do's and don'ts

How to avoid some of the pitfalls
that face the unwary traveller

The three hats game

Well-organized gangs operating beside busy streets or on squares lure tourists into parting with their cash. It is a time-honoured ruse involving one marble and three matchboxes or cups. Which 'hat' is the marble under? Try it and you are bound to lose. Make accusations of cheating and you could be in for a fight.

Strip clubs

The areas around Stuttgarter Platz, along Kantstrasse and along Potsdamer Strasse are not in themselves dangerous, but if you venture into one of the red-light establishments you are almost certain to be ripped off. The men who work in these clubs are not averse to strong-arm tactics, especially if you make trouble by complaining about the exorbitant bar prices.

Jaywalking

If you are the kind of pedestrian who will use the slightest break in the traffic to dash across the road, be warned: Germans do not usually do this. Berlin may be a fairly laid-back, even unconventional, city in many respects, but Berliners will still wait patiently for the 'green man' before crossing the road – even if there are no cars for as far as the eye can see. Jaywalking will earn you general disapproval from your fellow pedestrians – as well as a hefty on-the-spot fine from any police officer who sees you.

The Kurfürstendamm

The steamier side of Berlin's tourist trade is concentrated around the Kurfürstendamm. This is where most of the bars are, so motorists driving along this busy road and the even busier Lietzenburger Strasse after midnight need to watch out for inebriated groups of revellers stumbling back to their hotels.

Driving in the city centre

Every day, commercial and construction traffic brings the road between Potsdamer Platz and Moritzplatz to a standstill. In the Mitte district, Tiergarten, and elsewhere, road blocks and diversions arising from the major building work make the traffic gridlock even worse.

INDEX

This index lists the main places, sights and museums mentioned in this guide. Main entries are shown in bold, illustrations in italics.

What do you get for your money?

There is still something of a price gap between East and West Berlin. A meal in a basic restaurant will be no cheaper in the east than in the west, but a trip to the hairdressers will be, as will a visit to the cinema. However, there is now barely any difference in food, clothing, taxis, or in accommodation in the better-class hotels. Public transport costs the same anywhere; the cheapest single ticket is 3.60 DM. A visit to any of the museums of the Stiftung Preussischer Kulturbesitz will cost 4 DM, other museums 6 DM, special exhibitions 6 to 12 DM. A trip to the cinema costs between 8 and 15 DM. The cheapest theatre and opera tickets are around 10 DM in both eastern and western districts of the city. Better seats may cost 50 DM or more: at the Theater des Westens, a good seat can set you back 70 DM, and at the opera you may have to pay as much as 125 DM. Expect to pay between 50 and 70 DM for entry to rock or pop concerts if they feature international stars, and about the same for a good seat at one of the jazz festivals. A sightseeing tour will set you back 25–40 DM. Prices in bars and cafés vary a good deal, but 3 DM should buy you a beer or a coffee, between 5 and 9 DM a glass of wine.

£	DM	DM	£
1	2.90	1	0.34
2	5.80	2	0.69
3	8.70	3	1.03
4	11.60	4	1.38
5	14.50	5	1.72
10	29.00	10	3.45
20	58.00	20	6.90
30	87.00	30	10.34
40	116.00	40	13.79
50	145.00	50	17.24
60	174.00	60	20.69
70	203.00	70	24.14
80	232.00	80	27.59
90	261.00	90	31.03
100	290.00	100	34.48
200	580.00	200	68.97
250	725.00	250	86.21
500	1450.00	500	172.41
750	2175.00	750	262.50
1000	2900.00	1000	344.83

The conversion table above is based on the Thomas Cook sell rate, February 98

96